CLASS

This book aims to demonstrate the key importance of the concept of class in sociology. This is achieved by tracing the development of the class concept from the classic works of Marx and Weber to the more recent contributions of the neo-Marxist Wright and the neo-Weberian Goldthorpe, and by describing the class structures of contemporary Britain and the USA.

The book surveys the relevant literature on class, examines the question of how the class concept may be operationalized, and analyses class, social mobility, inequality and politics in both Britain and the USA. It also includes a discussion of the idea of a classless society. Each chapter ends with a clear summary of the argument and a review of the major theoretical conclusions.

The author suggests that there is an emergent convergence in Marxist and Weberian approaches to class, while at the same time providing a critique of both these perspectives. In addition, he assesses the thesis of American exceptionalism in the light of recent empirical research on the class system in the USA.

Wide-ranging, concise and user-friendly, this text will be of use to all students of sociology and politics from secondary school to undergraduate levels.

Stephen Edgell is Professor in Sociology at the University of Salford. He is the author of *Middle Class Couples* (1980) and co-author of *A Measure of Thatcherism* (1991).

KEY IDEAS
Series Editor: Peter Hamilton
The Open University

KEY IDEAS
Series Editor: PETER HAMILTON
The Open University, Milton Keynes

Designed to complement the successful *Key Sociologists*, this series covers the main concepts, issues, debates, and controversies in sociology and the social sciences. The series aims to provide authoritative essays on central topics of social science, such as community, power, work, sexuality, inequality, benefits and ideology, class, family, etc. Books adopt a strong individual 'line' constituting original essays rather than literary surveys, and form lively and original treatments of their subject matter. The books will be useful to students and teachers of sociology, political science, economics, psychology, philosophy, and geography.

THE SYMBOLIC CONSTRUCTION OF COMMUNITY
ANTHONY P. COHEN, Department of Social Anthropology, University of Manchester
SOCIETY
DAVID FRISBY and DEREK SAYER, Department of Sociology, University of Manchester
SEXUALITY
JEFFREY WEEKS, Social Work Studies Department, University of Southampton
WORKING
GRAEME SALAMAN, Faculty of Social Sciences, The Open University, Milton Keynes
BELIEFS AND IDEOLOGY
KENNETH THOMPSON, Faculty of Social Sciences, The Open University, Milton Keynes
EQUALITY
BRYAN TURNER, School of Social Sciences, The Flinders University of South Australia
HEGEMONY
ROBERT BOCOCK, Faculty of Social Sciences, The Open University, Milton Keynes
RACISM
ROBERT MILES, Department of Sociology, University of Glasgow
POSTMODERNITY
BARRY SMART, Associate Professor of Sociology, University of Auckland, New Zealand

CLASS

STEPHEN EDGELL

London and New York

First published 1993
by Routledge
11 New Fetter Lane, London EC4P 4EE

Simultaneously published in the USA and Canada
by Routledge
29 West 35th Street, New York, NY 10001

Reprinted 1994, 1995

© 1993 Stephen Edgell

Typeset in Times by Intype, London

Printed and bound in Great Britain by Clays Ltd., St. Ives PLC

British Cataloguing in Publication Data
A catalogue record for this book is available from the British Library

Library of Congress Cataloguing in Publication Data
A catalogue record for this book is available from the Library of
Congress

ISBN 0–415–06061–3

Contents

Illustrations

FIGURES

TABLES

Preface

In 1989 I reviewed a book entitled *Status* and noted in my review that this concept 'seems to have lived in the shadow of the concept class', yet this text 'appears in a series that does not contain a book on class in either its published or forthcoming titles' (Edgell 1989: 647). I was contacted subsequently by Chris Rojek, the senior sociology editor at Routledge, who referred to this book review in the context of his plans to publish a short book on class. This book is the outcome of our contact.

Stinchcombe has claimed that: 'Sociology has only one independent variable, class' (quoted in Wright 1979: 3). This is an extreme view but it is indicative of the importance of the most widely used concept in sociology. The primary reason for this is that class is thought to exercise an enormous influence on the ways in which an industrial capitalist society operates and develops. The extent of its influence can be seen by its frequent use in virtually every substantive area of sociology, including inequality, politics, education, health, family, work, consumption and leisure. Hence the thrust of the review was that class is a more important concept than status.

Probably more has been written about class than about any

other topic in sociology, and therefore it is not possible to cover the vast sociological literature on class in one short book, although such a book can be used as a selective guide to it. Moreover, from the large number of sources cited, a generous range of quotations has been selected to inform the reader of the precise location of a specific point and to enable her/him to check out the wider context.

The purpose of this study is to consider the centrality of the concept of class in sociology with special reference to what Mills (1967) has called the classic sociological tradition – the social analysis of historical social structures. The seminal contributions of Marx and Weber to the sociological understanding of class were written within this tradition. Thus, this study is not only a testimony to the enduring significance of the concept of class, it is also a celebration of the continued relevance of the Marxist and Weberian traditions of class analysis.

The essentially macro approach adopted in this study involves a discussion of changes in the class structure of whole societies, notably Britain and America, respectively the first and the most developed examples of industrial capitalism. This perspective treats class as a classificatory concept that can be used in theories concerned with propositions about observable regularities. Hence, for the purpose of class analysis, people who have something in common can be grouped together, whether or not they are aware of their common situation. Thus, it is not necessary for a person to be aware of class for it to have a profound impact on their everyday life:

> No matter what people believe, class structure as an economic arrangement influences their life chances according to their positions in it. If they do not grasp the causes of their conduct this does not mean that the social analyst must ignore or deny them.
>
> (Gerth and Mills 1961: 340)

Acknowledgements

Many of the ideas expressed in this book were developed during my collaborative research with Vic Duke on the social and political effects of Thatcherism. They were first published in our jointly authored articles in the *British Journal of Sociology* and in our book entitled *A Measure of Thatcherism: A Sociology of Britain*. I am grateful to the Editor of that journal and to Routledge for permission to reprint this material in revised form.

I would like to thank Vic Duke, Chris Bryant and Rob Flynn, all colleagues in the Department of Sociology, University of Salford, for their helpful comments on the first draft of various chapters, and Sheila Walker for typing the references. The usual disclaimers hold.

1

Classical theories of class: Marx and Weber

INTRODUCTION

Originally the term class referred to the division of the Roman population on the basis of property for fiscal and military purposes. This pre-modern usage was a static one in the sense that classes were regarded as ascriptive groupings of people who inherited a shared rank in society. The modern vocabulary of class is inextricably associated with the total reorganization of society that followed the industrial revolution. This change to what is nowadays called industrial capitalism or modern capitalism started in England in the late eighteenth century and spread during the following century to other western countries, notably France, Germany and America, and became a truly global phenomenon this century. Two of the major consequences of this momentous social change were the creation of new classes in a transformed class structure and the tendency for class positions to be allocated on the basis of ability rather than birth. Defining class and analysing class relationships in the context of a rapidly changing society became a central issue among founding sociologists, and controversies surrounding the concept of class have continued unabated to this day. The purpose of this chapter is to review and compare the two towering contributions of Marx (1818–83) and Weber (1864–1920) to the conceptualization and theorization of class.

MARX ON CLASS

Karl Marx was responsible for the first and one of the most important sociological theories of class. Its importance is due to its intellectual influence on subsequent theories of class and to its political influence on the revolutionary direction taken by certain societies inspired by his writings as a whole, and by his unfinished theory of class in particular (the chapter specifically on class in Capital III 'breaks off', 1974: 886). Thus, Marx's analysis of class represents an exercise in both theoretical and applied sociology.

However, Marx not only failed to elucidate systematically his use of the concept class and related concepts such as ruling class, he used them inconsistently – for example, middle class. In view of this, plus the tendency for Marxian ideas to be interpreted in a variety of ways, the *Dictionary of Marxist Thought* (Bottomore 1991) should be consulted whenever a Marxian term is encountered in this or any other text.

Marx's theory of class was part of a much broader and more ambitious account of nothing less than the history of all human societies, with special reference to the most recent stage of economic development, namely industrial capitalism. For Marx, what is 'new' about this mode of production (on the problematic nature of this concept see Bottomore 1991: 373–5) is its greater efficiency in creating 'surplus-value' or profit. In other words, it is a historically superior system of exploiting labour. Industrial capitalism is also particularly distinctive in its increasingly 'simplified' class system.

> Our epoch, the epoch of the bourgeoisie, possesses, however, this distinctive feature: it has simplified the class antagonisms. Society as a whole is more and more splitting up into two great hostile camps, into two great classes directly facing each other: Bourgeoisie and Proletariat.
>
> (Marx and Engels 1848: 49)

It was further argued that the class system of capitalism was 'simplified' in a second sense, namely that the relationship between dominant and subordinate classes was more instrumental and impersonal than in the past.

> The bourgeoisie, wherever it has got the upper hand, has put an end to all feudal, patriarchal, idyllic relations. It has pitilessly torn asunder the motley feudal ties that bound man to his 'natural superiors', and has left remaining no other nexus between man and man than naked self-interest, than callous 'cash payment.' . . . In one word, for exploitation, veiled by religious and political illusions, it has substituted naked, shameless, direct, brutal exploitation.
>
> (Marx and Engels 1848: 52)

These two key passages are from the *Manifesto of the Communist Party* which was first published in a year of widespread political unrest in Europe. Allowing for the less than sober language of this essentially agitational rather than analytical tract, the pamphlet as a whole provides, as these quotes illustrate, a good guide to the basic ideas that comprise Marx's theory of class.

The reason why Marx claims that there are only two major classes under capitalism is that since private property was now the basis of economic relations, there were logically only two possibilities; a class who own the means of production and a class who do not and hence have to sell their capacity to work ('labour-power' in Marx's terminology). And the reason why relations between employers and employees are inherently 'antagonistic' is that in order to make a profit and survive in a competitive economic situation, the former are constrained to 'exploit' the latter. Moreover, in the process of extracting 'surplus-labour', the employer is not only concerned to keep costs as low as possible by paying the minimum necessary to attract and retain workers, but also seeks to achieve the highest attainable level of production. Hence, profits and wages are inversely related, and 'the interests of capital and the interests of labour are diametrically opposed' (Marx 1952: 36). There is therefore an inevitable conflict between the two main social classes over the price of labour and the labour process or productive system. Marx recognized that both the bourgeoisie and the proletariat are divided by competition among themselves, but become united in their opposition to each other. According to Marx, the effect of this structure of class relations was an increasingly large, poor, homo-

genized and alienated work force compared to a smaller yet far
wealthier class of employers. Marx thought that the final outcome
of this polarization would be revolutionary class conflict, and that
victory for the working classes was inevitable.

It is apparent from these few introductory statements that
Marx's theory of class is fundamentally a dynamic conception of
class and that the motor of social change is conflict. Indeed, class
conflict is the key element in Marx's account of the history of
all societies, not just of the origins, development and future of
capitalism. In the case of the transition from feudalism to capitalism, the urban bourgeoisie or manufacturing middle class played
the revolutionary role, pushing aside the monopolistic guild masters and eventually displacing by force the ruling landed aristocracy. Thus Marx argued that the bourgeoisie became the ruling
class in the new type of society – capitalism – by combining
together and engaging in revolutionary class conflict.

Marx acknowledged the achievements of the now dominant
capitalist class, who had not only overthrown the feudal lords
and their limited economic system of production, but went on to
transform the economic and social structure of capitalism in a
relatively short period of time. For example, the bourgeoisie had
revolutionized the means of production, concentrated workers in
large factories located in huge cities, created a world market,
and above all, produced goods on a scale and of a cheapness
hitherto unknown, indeed, unimaginable.

> The bourgeoisie, during its rule of scarce one hundred
> years, has created more massive and more colossal pro-
> ductive forces than have all preceding generations
> together.
>
> (Marx and Engels 1848: 57)

However, for Marx the advantages of capitalism were exceeded
by its disadvantages. He claimed that the capitalist mode of
production was an 'anarchical system of competition' characterized by 'the most outrageous squandering of labour-power' and
periodic crises in which 'larger capitals beat the smaller' (Marx
1970a: 530 and 626). In these circumstances, the bourgeoisie
attempt to solve crises by destroying commodities (the 'absurdity'
of over-production), reducing staff, cutting wages and increasing
the intensity of labour, and by developing new markets and
exploiting old ones more thoroughly, for example via a credit
system. For Marx, such solutions may restore equilibrium in the

short run, but in the longer term they merely pave the way for bigger and deeper crises.

In addition to creating an inherently unstable economic system, Marx argues that the bourgeoisie have also created the class that will effect its ultimate downfall, the proletariat.

> But not only has the bourgeoisie forged the weapons that bring death to itself; it has also called into existence the men who are to wield those weapons – the modern working class – the proletarians.
>
> (Marx and Engels 1848: 60)

Thus, economic crises, however acute and frequent, do not guarantee the end of capitalism, they are simply the preconditions for revolutionary change. According to Marx, it is only through the class action of the proletariat that capitalist society will be transcended.

PROLETARIANIZATION, POLARIZATION AND REVOLUTIONARY CHANGE

The self-destructive nature of industrial capitalism is ensured by the important social process of proletarianization, which facilitates the historical revolutionary role that Marx assigned to the working class. For Marx, proletarianization specifically refers to a change from self-employment to employee status, but three meanings are discernible in his writings:

1 the proletarianization of society
2 the proletarianization of work and
3 political proletarianization.

First, the proletarianization of society refers to the tendency for the working class to increase in size, to be concentrated in large factories in urban areas and to experience relative poverty as a result of the development of the capitalist mode of production. Marx claimed that one of the 'laws' of capitalist development was that the competitive nature of capitalist industrialization favoured big capital at the expense of small capital and resulted in the concentration of the ownership of capital. As a consequence, the self-employed and small-scale owners go out of business, and become increasingly impoverished wage labourers.

The lower strata of the middle class – the small trades-people, shopkeepers, and retired tradesmen generally, the handicraftsmen and peasants – all sink gradually into the proletariat, partly because their diminutive capital does not suffice for the scale on which Modern Industry is carried on, and is swamped in the competition with the large capitalists, partly because their specialized skill is rendered worthless by the new methods of production . . . In proportion as capital accumulates, the lot of the labourer, be his payment high or low, must get worse.

(Marx and Engels 1848: 62 and Marx 1970a: 645)

Second, upon becoming wage labourers (or wage slaves in Marx's terminology), the new recruits to the proletariat become 'enslaved' by the production process, including the machine, the supervisor and the employer. Marx argued that under capitalism workers are treated just like any other commodity, to be bought and sold in the market place for the lowest possible price. Moreover, owing to the increased use of machinery (i.e. dead labour in Marx's terminology), plus the specialized division of labour, work becomes deskilled and workers become degraded as they lose all autonomy and individuality. This dimension of proletarianization is part of Marx's famous alienation thesis, which is more fully theorized in his *Economic and Philosophical Manuscripts of 1844* (1970b), and described in great detail in Volume 1 of *Capital* (1970a). However, the neatest summary of the proletarianization of work can be found yet again in the *Manifesto of the Communist Party*.

[The worker] becomes an appendage of the machine, and it is only the most simple, most monotonous, and most easily acquired knack, that is required of him . . . Masses of labourers, crowded into the factory are organised like soldiers. As privates of the industrial army they are placed under the command of a perfect hierarchy of officers and sergeants.

(Marx and Engels 1848: 60 and 61)

The third and final sense in which Marx uses the term proletarianization is to refer to the growth of working class political consciousness. This is arguably the most crucial, complex and controversial dimension of proletarianization. Marx argued that once the proletariat has increased in size, concentration and relative poverty, and experienced degradation at work, workers will join together to defend and/or improve their wages and working conditions: in other words, come into class conflict with the bourgeoisie. The collective power of workers will be enhanced by victories initially at the local level, but with the improvement of the means of communication created by industrialization, class struggles will develop on a national scale. In order for the political consciousness of the working classes to grow to the point at which they can challenge successfully the domination of the capitalist class, the proletariat has to organize at work (i.e. form trade unions) and outside of work (i.e. form a political party). Eventually, notwithstanding temporary setbacks, clashes between the proletariat and the ruling capitalist class, in their attempts to defend and/or advance their respective material interests, would reach a revolutionary pitch. Marx was confident that at this stage the proletariat would prevail and establish a new type of society which was free of exploitation and oppression, i.e. classless.

> Economic conditions had first transformed the mass of the people of the country into workers. The combination of capital has created for this mass a common situation, common interests. This mass is thus already a class as against capital, but not yet for itself. In the struggle . . . this mass becomes united, and constitutes itself as a class for itself. The interests it defends become class interests. But the struggle of class against class is a political struggle . . . [Eventually class] war breaks out into open revolution . . . the violent overthrow of the bourgeoisie lays the foundation for the sway of the proletariat . . . in which the free development of each is the condition for the free development of all.
>
> (Marx 1971: 173 and Marx and Engels 1848: 70 and 90)

This outline of Marx's theory of class in modern capitalist societies represents a summary of his basic proletarianization–radicalization–revolution thesis, in which the class structure polarizes into two internally homogeneous classes who engage in ever increasing degrees of conflict. That Marx considered this thesis to be the essence of capitalism is not surprising.

Marx was no mere theorist. In the first place he considered that the whole purpose of his lifework was to help to change society for the better as he saw it, and not simply study it for its own sake (Marx and Engels 1970).

Second, Marx was active in radical politics all his life: he experienced the turbulence of revolt and repression in Europe, especially during the revolutions of 1848, and ended up a political refugee in England by the 1850s (Berlin, 1963).

Third, Marx's empirical reference point for his theory of class was nineteenth-century England, the first industrial capitalist society, though he was not unaware of the capitalist development of countries such as France and America. Marx lived and worked in poverty in England for over thirty years and was impressed by the immense wealth being produced, the manner of its production, the inequality of its distribution and the extensive and extreme class conflict this situation engendered. More specifically, Marx observed, studied and was part of the great contrast and conflictual relationship between the affluence, splendour and power of the capitalist class, and the poverty, degradation and powerlessness of the working class. For example, he documented the acute poverty of the English agricultural labourer at the beginning of the nineteenth century and contrasted it with the way in which the bourgeoisie 'had enriched themselves so extraordinarily' during the same period (1970a: 674). He concluded that this structure of inequality and related pattern of conflict was unavoidable under capitalism and that revolution was the only way to overcome it.

In view of the evidence all around him, and given his political commitment to revolutionary social change, it is little wonder that he conceptualized class in essentially dichotomous and conflictual terms.

IMPEDIMENTS TO REVOLUTIONARY CHANGE

In addition to advancing a theory about the transformation of industrial capitalism on the basis of the inherent conflict of class interests, Marx also noted that relationships within and between classes were far more complex, and therefore problematic, than his dichotomous model implied, and that they represented potential impediments to class formation, conflict and therefore total change.

The first complication that could hinder progress towards revolutionary change is that there are often more classes than the two main ones noted thus far. Marx referred to many other

classes, plus factions or fractions of classes, in various works, but
most notably in *The Eighteenth Brumaire of Louis Bonaparte*
(1972). In this detailed analysis of mid-nineteenth century France,
Marx discusses class fractions within the two major social classes:
capital, e.g. landed, financial and industrial, and labour, e.g.
lumpenproletariat and proletariat; two transitional classes: petty
bourgeoisie and peasantry; plus several middle classes e.g. 'the
high dignitaries of the army, the university, the church, the bar,
the academy, and of the press' (1972: 28). Elsewhere Marx also
wrote about the aristocracy of labour, the best-paid section of
the working class and often mentioned other divisions within the
working class based on age, sex, skill, and the contrast between
rural and urban workers (1970a). He also used the terms lower
middle class and middle class to refer to the self-employed and
small-scale capitalists (Marx and Engels 1848). Finally, Marx was
also aware of the growth of the propertyless middle classes 'who
stand between the workman on the one hand and the capitalist
and landlord on the other' (1969: 573). For Marx (and Engels)
it was 'the universal competitive struggle' that caused classes to
fragment as well as coalesce: 'Competition separates individuals
from one another, not only the bourgeois but still more the
workers, in spite of the fact that it brings them together' (1970:
79). Consequently, the precise structure of class relationships, at
any one time and place, depends upon the circumstances. For
instance, at a time of acute political conflict the class structure is
likely to be highly polarized. Thus, class polarization and class
fragmentation are a matter of degree. Obviously, competition
and political disunity among capitalists is good news from the
standpoint of the proletariat, and vice versa. In other words,
Marx's two conflicting classes theory does not rule out the possibility of the existence of many classes and fractions, and all that
this implies in terms of variations in class consciousness and
action.

The second important complication that could impede the
process whereby a class is transformed from an economic interest
group into a politically active revolutionary force concerns the
integrative role of ideology. This refers to Marx's thesis that the
dominant capitalist class not only controls the means of material
production (things), but also controls the means of mental production (ideas). Thus every ruling class throughout history

is compelled, merely in order to carry through its aim,

to present its interests as the common interest of all the members of society . . . it has to give its ideas the form of universality, and represent them as the only rational, universally valid ones.

(Marx and Engels 1970: 65–6)

Marx used the phrase 'hegemony of the spirit' (Marx and Engels 1970: 67), whereas it is now commonplace, following Gramsci (1971), to describe the consensual dimension of ruling-class domination as hegemony (Bottomore 1991).

An additional and related obstacle to full class consciousness and the revolutionary overthrow of capitalism concerns the pervasiveness of the 'fetishism of commodities' in which social relations between people appear 'in the fantastic form of a relation between things' (Marx 1970a: 72). Marx meant by this the tendency for workers in the alienating capitalist mode of production to focus on the acquisition of commodities as an end in itself rather than on their usefulness. The political implication of this tendency is that the workers' fetish for commodities distracts them from the fight against the domination of capital.

Thus Marx recognized that revolutionary change via capitalist economic crises and working-class political action was fraught with difficulties. This point was conceded when he wrote of the 'law' of capitalist development: 'Like all other laws it is modified in its working by many circumstances' (1970a: 644). Marx's two major conflicting classes model, based on his theories of exploitation, proletarianization and polarization, led him both to expect and hope that revolutionary change would lead to the abolition of private property and the inauguration of a classless society. However, the failure of the working classes of advanced capitalist societies to conform to Marx's theoretical and political expectations suggests that class fragmentation is more pervasive historically than class polarization, and that Marx seriously underestimated the ability of capitalist societies to contain class conflict and prosper.

Some sociologists have concluded that Marx's conception of a capitalist society polarized into two conflicting classes is obsolete (e.g. Dahrendorf 1964; Parkin 1979). In other words, this model may well have been an accurate account of class in the nineteenth century, but it is increasingly inapplicable in this century. Typically, it is argued that not only has revolutionary change failed to occur, but that the middle class has expanded in size at the expense of the working class – proletarianization in reverse. History seems to have refuted Marx. Those who express this view tend to be more sympathetic to Weber's analysis of class, which is the subject of the next section.

WEBER ON CLASS

Max Weber is credited with developing Marx's theory of class in the broader context of what has since become known as social stratification, i.e. the division of a society into a number of hierarchically arranged strata. Consequently, in contrast to Marx, Weber drew attention to other forms of stratification other than class, notably status and ethnic stratification. However, in the following account of Weber's contribution to the sociology of class, non-class groupings will be mentioned only when they are directly relevant to class analysis. There are many texts which provide an overview of Weber's wider concern with social stratification, some quite brief and of necessity elementary (e.g. Saunders 1990) and others much longer and more detailed (e.g. Giddens 1979).

A further important contrast between Marx and Weber's approach to class is that this concept plays a minor role in Weber's encyclopedic sociology. Yet, ironically, within this more limited appreciation of class Weber, unlike Marx, provides a sytematic discussion of the concept of class. However, in the two places where Weber considers class, the translators and editors, Gerth and Mills, and Parsons respectively, note that the manuscript breaks off (Weber 1961 and 1964). These key passages can be found elsewhere (Weber 1968a and 1968b), though the translation by Roth and Wittich differs slightly. In other words, Weber's account of class is incomplete, just like Marx's!

The concept of class has long been recognized as a highly political one, especially in the hands of Marx the revolutionary socialist. In fact, Lipset and Bendix have suggested that: 'Discussions of different theories of class are often academic substitutes for real conflict over political orientations' (1951: 150). In this context it is pertinent to say something about Weber's political views, prior to outlining his contribution to the sociology of class.

In contrast to Marx's well-known critique and opposition to industrial capitalism, Weber approved of the rationality of modern capitalism and was opposed to socialism. Essentially,

Weber thought that bureaucracy was more efficient than any other form of administration and that modern capitalism favoured its development.

> It is superior to any other form in precision, in stability, in the stringency of its discipline, and in its reliability . . .
> Capitalism is the most rational economic basis for bureaucratic administration and enables it to develop in the most rational form.
>
> (Weber 1968a: 223 and 224)

Moreover, although Weber expressed fears about the difficulty of escaping from an increasingly depersonalized and mechanized bureaucratic world (Weber 1968c), he thought that socialism would weaken the incentive to work and exacerbate the dehumanizing consequences of bureaucratization (Weber 1968a). Thus, Weber was an admirer, albeit a critical one, of modern capitalism and its characteristic form of organization, the legal-rational bureaucracy.

Weber contended that class refers to any group of people who share a common class situation, which he defined as:

> The typical chance for a supply of goods, external living conditions, and personal life experiences, in so far as this chance is determined by the amount and kind of power, or lack of such, to dispose of goods or skills for the sake of income in a given economic order.
>
> (Weber 1961: 181)

Thus, for Weber, 'the kind of chance in the market is the decisive moment which presents a common condition for the individual's fate' (1961: 182).

On the basis of this definition of class Weber distinguished between two types of positively privileged classes, namely owner-ship or property classes and acquisition or commercial classes. The former comprise those who own different kinds of property, e.g. land, buildings and people; and the latter includes all those who possess goods, services and skills that can be offered on the market, e.g. industrial and agricultural entrepreneurs, merchants, bankers, professionals and 'workers with monopolistic qualifi-cations and skills' (Weber 1968a: 303 and 304). Weber also distin-guished between three types of negatively privileged property classes, namely, 'the unfree, the declassed and the "paupers"' and three types of negatively privileged commercial classes, namely, skilled, semi-skilled and unskilled workers (1968a: 303 and 304). In between both types of positively and negatively privileged classes Weber noted the existence of various 'middle classes', e.g. peasants, craftsmen, public and private officials, liberal professions and groups of workers with exceptional credentials and/or skills (Weber 1968a: 303 and 304). In addition, Weber discussed the constellation of class situations that he referred to as social classes: 'A "social class" makes up the totality of those class situations within which individual and generational mobility is easy and typical' (1968a: 302). Weber listed four such groupings; the working class as a whole, the petty bourgeoisie, the propertyless intelligentsia and specialists such as technicians, and 'classes privileged through property and education' (1968a: 305). Weber also distinguished between class and status situations, but noted that 'class situation is by far the predominant factor' in modern society (1961: 190).

Thus, according to Weber, class was essentially an economic phenomenon; more precisely, it was determined by a person's market situation. Moreover, Weber claimed that 'property' and 'lack of property' were the 'basic categories of all class situations' (1961: 182). However, since Weber not only analysed different forms of social stratification, but differentiated between a number of positively privileged classes, negatively privileged classes and middle classes, and distinguished between class situations and constellations of class situations, his conception of the social stratification structure in general, and the class structure in particular, is extremely complex and pluralistic.

THE FRAGMENTATION OF CLASS CONFLICT

Whilst Weber did not advance a general theory of class change, apart, that is, from noting that he expected the petty bourgeoisie to decline and white-collar workers to expand with the development of industrial capitalism (1968a: 305), he did discuss class divisions and conflict.

Weber claimed that the 'factor that creates "class" is unambiguously economic interest . . . Nevertheless, the concept of "class-interest" is an ambiguous one' (1961: 183). This is because

the direction of interests may vary according to whether or not a communal action of a larger or smaller portion of those commonly affected by the "class situation", or even an association among them, e.g. a "trade union", has grown out of the class situation from which the individual may or may not expect promising results.

(Weber 1961: 183)

Furthermore, organized class action is facilitated by certain conditions, including 'the possibility of concentrating on opponents where the immediate conflict of interests is vital' and where large classes are concentrated, e.g. workers against managers in a large factory (Weber 1964: 427). Thus, for Weber, the relationship between class, economic interests and class action is not as staightforward as a certain 'talented author' would have us believe (1961: 185).

The issue of class action is also complicated by the existence of status groups based on the 'positive or negative, social estimation of honor' (Weber 1961: 187). Weber argued that since 'parties may represent interests determined through "class situation" or "status situation", they may recruit their following respectively from one or the other', or 'neither' (1961: 194).

Thus, Weber's sociology of class starts with two 'basic categories of all class situations', namely property and propertylessness, but differentiates a large number of both positively and negatively privileged classes with reference to education as well as property, and includes an analysis of status groups (1961: 182). This essentially hierarchical and highly pluralistic account of class (and status) recognized that economic interests were at the root of class action, but also recognized that the expression of class interests was problematic, not least because of the variable connections between class and status, especially in relation to parties.

SUMMARY AND CONCLUSIONS

Marx and Weber conceptualized class in economic terms and claimed that the main class categories in modern capitalism involved the distinction between the ownership and the non-ownership of property for exchange, and differentiated a variety of other classes. Hence their views on class overlap in important ways, although there are also clear differences in emphasis. For example, Weber stressed more than Marx the class advantages that flowed from knowledge or skills, and he also distinguished class situations from status situations, but noted that the former were more important than the latter in modern society. More-

over, Marx concentrated on the role of conflict and the polarization of the class structure, whereas Weber focused on the problematic nature of class action and the fragmentation of the class
structure. Marx concluded that socialism would overcome the
inherently conflictual nature of capitalism and inaugurate a classless society. Weber, on the other hand, whilst he was concerned
about the dehumanizing potential of 'rational' capitalism, claimed
that socialism would only make things worse. Finally, although
class plays a starring role in Marx's sociology and a less prominent
one in Weber's, following Giddens (1979), it may be suggested
that together they provide the essential conceptual tools for analysing contemporary class structures, namely the economic factors
that give rise to classes: the ownership of property and the possession of knowledge and physical labour power.

2

Contemporary theories of class: neo-Marxist and neo-Weberian

INTRODUCTION

The theoretical dominance of Marx and Weber's accounts of the meaning of class is reflected in the continuity between their perspectives and in virtually all subsequent attempts to understand the key concept of class. The purpose of this chapter is to consider Wright's neo-Marxist theory of class and Goldthorpe's neo-Weberian theory of class. These contemporary accounts of class were selected because they have influenced the development of class schemes that have been used in recent empirical research. More specifically, Wright's contribution involved a revision of Marx's model of class and has been operationalized successfully in sociological studies of the American, Swedish and British class structures (e.g. Wright 1985; Edgell and Duke 1991). By the same token, Goldthorpe's contribution involved a revision of Weber's model of class and has been used in recent studies of class in Britain and other modern industrial societies (e.g. Goldthorpe 1987; Marshall *et al*. 1988; Erikson and Goldthorpe 1992). Hence, Wright and Goldthorpe represent the two major theoretical traditions of class analysis, the Marxian and Weberian respectively.

Others have written within these traditions, but their theories have not been tested in the field to the same extent as Wright and Goldthorpe (e.g. the neo-Marxists Carchedi 1977 and Poulantzas 1979, and the neo-Weberians Giddens 1979 and Parkin 1979).

WRIGHT'S NEO-MARXIST THEORY OF CLASS

Wright is a reflexive American neo-Marxist sociologist who has been revising his reformulation of Marx's original theory of class continually since the mid 1970s. His starting point was that Marxism has been more influential theoretically than empirically, notwithstanding the many modifications to the Marxist theory of class formulated by European Marxists. He is therefore concerned to develop a Marxian typology of classes that can be used in empirical research. According to Wright:

> It matters a great deal for our understanding of class struggle and social change exactly how classes are conceptualized and which categories of social positions are placed in which classes.
>
> (Wright 1976: 3–4).

Wright's first 'class map' was developed in his Ph.D dissertation, which was subsequently published in book form (1979). At this early stage of his class research, Wright picked up the idea of 'contradictory class locations' from the work of Carchedi on the problem of understanding the 'new middle class' in advanced capitalist societies. He notes that in one sense 'all class positions are "contradictory locations", since all class relations are intrinsically antagonistic, but some positions in the class structure are doubly so because they represent positions which are torn between the basic contradictory class relations of capitalist society' (1976: 26). Wright called these ambiguous classes contradictory classes in preference to the inelegant term 'contradictory locations within the basic contradictory class locations'. This idea enabled Wright to theorize the problematic middle classes and expand the basic Marxian dichotomous class model to include managers, small employers and semi-autonomous wage earners.

Thus, for Wright, managers are in a contradictory location between the bourgeoisie and the proletariat, semi-autonomous workers occupy a contradictory location between the petty bourgeoisie and the proletariat, and small employers occupy a contradictory location between the bourgeoisie and the petty

Figure 2.1 Wright: class map I (basic version): the relationship of contradictory class locations to the basic class forces in capitalist society

BOURGEOISIE

                       Small employers

   Managers   PETTY BOURGEOISIE

                  Semi-autonomous workers

PROLETARIAT

Note: Classes are in upper case, contradictory locations within class relations in lower case.
Source: Wright 1976: 27

bourgeoisie. The basis of Wright's differentiation of these three contradictory class locations was the concept of control; control over investment and the accumulation process, control over the means of production, and control of labour power. In an advanced capitalist society, the bourgeoisie enjoy all three types of control and the proletariat none. The petty bourgeoisie are similar to the bourgeoisie except that they do not control the labour power of others. Managers, small employers and semi-autonomous workers enjoy varying amounts of control, more than workers but less than the bourgeoisie. Thus, contradictory classes are those who exhibit a mixed pattern of control.

In his more detailed account of the concept of control, Wright distinguishes between four degrees of control (full, partial, minimal and none), in addition to the three types of control noted above (1976: 33). This enabled him to differentiate four contradictory locations rather than one between the bourgeoisie and the proletariat, namely top managers who have minimal control over investments, middle managers who have partial control over investments, the means of production and the labour power of others, technocrats who have minimal control over production and labour, and foremen/line supervisors who have minimal control solely over labour. Wright also divided the bourgeoisie into the traditional capitalist and top corporate executives, on the grounds that the latter may own some rather than a lot of capital but do not enjoy the legal status of being an employer of labour, a sort of quasi-contradictory location. This recognition by Wright of the complexity of class relations means that his first class map contains between six and ten classes.

Figure 2.2 Wright: class map I (full version)

1. BOURGEOISIE: traditional capitalist
2. Quasi-contradictory location: top corporate executive
3. Contradictory location: top managers
4. Contradictory location: middle managers
5. Contradictory location: technocrats
6. Contradictory location: foremen/line supervisors
7. PROLETARIAT
8. Contradictory location: semi-autonomous workers
9. PETTY BOURGEOISIE
10. SMALL EMPLOYERS

Source: Wright 1976: 33

When he attempted to operationalize this class typology using survey data Wright found it 'impossible to define the contradictory class position between the petty bourgeoisie and the proletariat', because the class situation of semi-autonomous workers was virtually indistinguishable from that of the working class (Wright 1979: 241–2). Consequently, Wright merged this class with the proletariat, thereby abandoning the category of semi-autonomous workers (see also Wright 1985: 49–57). This heralded a move away from the concept of contradictory locations.

Although Wright thought that the concept of contradictory class location was an improvement on other attempts to deal with the issue of the propertyless middle class in advanced capitalist societies, he was aware of two other major difficulties. First, the term contradiction is inherently problematic because, except in the case of contradictory locations within the mode of production (the managers), the contradictory locations between modes of production 'are not obviously "contradictory" locations', but merely dual or mixed locations (Wright 1985: 53). Second, and in Wright's view, most important of all, 'the concept of contradictory class locations within class relations rested almost exclusively on relations of domination rather than exploitation' (1985: 56). For example, managers were defined by Wright as a contradictory location because they simultaneously dominated workers and were dominated by capitalists. Wright is highly critical of the marginalization of exploitation because it weakens the relationship between class position and class interests that is fundamental to classical Marxism and leads to a 'multiple oppressions' approach to social divisions (1985: 57). Wright's autocritique of the theoretical foundations of his first class map acknowledged many of the criticisms that had been levelled against the concept of contradictory class location (e.g. Giddens 1979; Stewart *et al*. 1980; Holmwood and Stewart 1983), and paved the way for a complete revision of his approach to class.

Wright drew upon Roemer's (1982) account of exploitation as 'the basis for elaborating a comprehensive framework for analysing class structure in general and for reconceptualizing the problem of the middle classes in particular' (1985: 73). Wright defined exploitation as 'an economically oppressive appropriation of the fruits of the labour of one class by another' (1985: 77), and argued that, in addition to capitalists who are able to exploit workers on the basis of their ownership of the means of production, certain non-owners are able to exploit other non-owners on the basis of their organizational assets and/or their skill/credential assets. By distinguishing between these three types of exploitation and combinations of them, Wright was able to develop a class scheme that remained faithful to the classical Marxian idea of exploitation, and associated dichotomy of owners and non-owners, yet reflected the increased complexity of class relations in advanced capitalism.

Wright's second class map can be looked at in two ways: first there is the division between the owners of the means of production and the non-owners, the primary structural class cleavage of capitalism; second, each basic class category is internally differentiated, the former in terms of whether or not the owner works and/or hires workers, the latter according to the type and degree of organizational and skill/credential assets the non-owners possess. This produces twelve classes, exactly double the number contained in his first basic class map. However, all the extra classes are located within the propertyless part of the class structure. Hence, Wright's class map II is reminiscent of the ten-class full version of class map I in the sense that it represents a more thoroughly theorized account of the complexities of the structure of class relations characteristic of modern capitalism.

In addition to this general advantage, Wright claims that his

Figure 2.3 Wright: class map II

Assets in the means of production

	Owners of means of production	Non-owners [wage labourers]		
			Organization assets	
		+	>0	–
Owns sufficient capital to hire workers and not work	1 Bourgeoisie	4 Expert managers	7 Semi-credentialled managers	10 Uncredentialled managers	+
Owns sufficient capital to hire workers but must work	2 Small employers	5 Expert supervisors	8 Semi-credentialled supervisors	11 Uncredentialled supervisors	>0 *Skill/credential assets*
Owns sufficient capital to work for self but not to hire workers	3 Petty bourgeoisie	6 Expert non-managers	9 Semi-credentialled workers	12 Proletarians	–

Source: Wright 1985: 88

reformulation of class is an improvement on his first class map since it recognizes that the propertyless middle classes

> have interests opposed to workers because of their effec-
> tive control of organization and skill assets. Within the
> struggles of capitalism, therefore, these 'new' middle
> classes do constitute contradictory locations, or more pre-
> cisely, contradictory locations within exploitative
> relations.
>
> (1985: 87)

Wright also argues that his revised class framework reveals which contradictory locations are the most important ones historically. He claims that within capitalism, the key contradictory location 'is constituted by managers and state bureaucrats' because these classes 'embody a principle of class organization which is quite distinct from capitalism and which potentially poses an alternative to capitalist relations' (1985: 89). In fact, he suggests that this applies more to state managers than to corporate managers, since the careers of the former are less tied in with the interests of the capitalist class.

Wright is quite open about the political implications of his second class map, although they fly in the face of the classical Marxian thesis concerning the historical revolutionary role of the proletariat. He admits that his reconceptualization of the propertyless middle class involves the possibility that in addition to the working class, 'there are other class forces within capitalism that have the potential to pose an alternative to capitalism', notably bureaucratic managers (1985: 89). Wright is similarly frank about the sociological consequences of this class map when he concedes that 'the process of class formation and class struggle is considerably more complex and indeterminate than the tra-ditional Marxist story has allowed' (1985: 91). Thus, Wright's second class map involves a major revision of Marx's sociology of class and its associated political expectations.

A CRITIQUE OF WRIGHT

Wright's penchant for critical reflection is evident in his discussion of the many problems generated by his second class map. He lists four main difficulties, all of which relate to his core concept of exploitation. First, he expresses doubts about organization exploitation on the grounds that: 'Even if one accepts the claim that managers and bureaucrats are exploiters, one might still be sceptical of the argument that the basis of their exploitation is control' (1985: 92). Second, he questions the relationship between skill exploitation and class when he notes that this type of exploitation may be the basis of intra-class divisions rather than inter-class divisions. Third, he is unsure about the links between the different types of exploitation, e.g. he regards the assumption that different types of exploitation reinforce each other as empirically implausible. Fourth and finally, he raises the issue of non-class bases of exploitation such as race, religion and sex, and argues that 'production-based exploitation [is] a distinct category from non-production exploitations because of the specific type of interdependency it creates between the exploited and the exploiter' (1985: 98).

Other sociologists have not been slow to build upon Wright's autocritique of his attempts to update Marx's theory of class. All are agreed that his latest revisions involve a move in the direction of Weber's conceptualization of class and away from Marx's (e.g. Giddens 1985; Carter 1986; Rose and Marshall 1986). For example, Weber not only emphasized the relevance of scarce skills and expertise to class analysis, and therefore the distinctiveness of the propertyless middle classes, but also stressed the role of non-class factors such as ethnic status. Wright anticipated this line of criticism and concluded that his own approach is still essentially 'materialist' and hence Marxian, and not 'culturalist' and therefore Weberian (1985: 108).

Wright's argument behind his defence against the accusation that his approach is no longer Marxist is that although Weberians use some of the same class criteria:

> In the Marxist framework, the material interests embedded in these processes of exploitation have an objective character regardless of the subjective states of the actors; in the Weberian perspective, it is only because rationalization implies a particular kind of subjective understanding of material interests by actors that one is justified in describing these relations as class relations at all.
> (Wright 1985: 108)

In other words, the increasing convergence between Wright's revisions of the Marxian conceptualization of class and Weberian class analysis is more apparent than real. But is it? Throughout his work Wright has outlined, sometimes briefly (e.g. 1979: 17), and on other occasions in more detail (e.g. 1985: 26-7), what constitues the general Marxist theory of class. These defining features can be summarized as follows (1979: 17):

1 Class is defined 'in relational rather than gradational terms'.
2 'The central axis of class relations is located within the social organization of production rather than the market'.
3 The analysis of class relations is rooted 'in an examination of the processes of exploitation rather than either the technical division of labour or authority relations'.

Notwithstanding the interrelatedness of these three points, each one can be treated as if they were separate analytically. The first alludes to the basic Marxist contention that class refers to relationships to the means of production and not to gradations of income, status, education and so on. Although classes defined in relation to other classes also possess gradational properties such as wealth, the crux of the issue is that it is not their distributional features which define class, but their relational character. All Wright's class maps are relational to the extent that they contain at their core the classical Marxist antagonistic class dichotomy, capitalists and workers. However, in elaborating his various class maps, he slips in a gradational element – for instance, in the fuller version of class map I, the distinction between top managers and middle managers is based on their degree of control within the capitalist hierarchy. Wright's use of the language of gradational class merely confirms that he is resorting to gradational factors to differentiate these contradictory classes.

A similar line of criticism applies to Wright's class map II, despite the change from a domination-centred class model to an exploitation-centred one. More specifically, whilst ownership exploitation is relational, organizational and skill/credential assets are arguably not relational but gradational. For example, it is not clear why the possession of skills and/or credentials should lead to the exploitation of non-experts by experts rather than to gradations of income. Wright effectively concedes this point by resorting once again to gradational language. Thus, the internal differentiation of non-owners is achieved by distinguishing between degrees of organizational and skill/credential assets. Perhaps the propertyless middle classes should be regarded as gradational class fractions, not as a distinctive relationally-defined class, a possibility that Wright mentions but does not consider in detail (1985: 95).

Wright's second defining feature of a Marxist theory of class involves the assertion that class is a production-centred, as well as a relational, concept. There are two problems with this issue, both of which are recognized by Wright. First, he notes that among Marxists there is no agreement about how to define the social relations of production – for example, in terms of property relations alone or in conjunction with other factors such as organizational assets (1985: 37). Second, he accepts that both Weber and Marx used production-based definitions of class: 'Capital, raw labour power and skills in Weber; capital and labour power in Marx' (1985: 107). According to Wright:

> The difference between them is that Weber views production from the vantage point of the market exchanges in which these assets are traded, whereas Marx views production from the vantage point of the exploitation it generates.
>
> (1985: 107).

Given that Wright has expanded his notion of exploitation to include two types other than that based on the ownership of private property, namely organization and skill/credential exploitation, his current position is effectively identical to that of Weber. This is because in addition to concurring with Marx that 'property and lack of property are . . . the basic categories of all class situations' (1961: 182), Weber argued that other factors, such as skill, can also create class differences among the propertyless. Thus it is difficult to see how Wright's revised scheme differs in practice from Weber's conceptualization of class with respect to the issue of production-based versus market-based definitions of class. However, in the final analysis, much depends on how social relations of production and the market are defined, and on one's interpretation of the Marxian and Weberian perspectives regarding this aspect of class (Crompton and Gubbay 1977).

Wright's third and final essential characteristic of the Marxist theory of class concerns the distinction between class and occupation. Marx and neo-Marxists, including Wright, place great emphasis on the exploitative production relations conception of class, in contrast to non-Marxist occupational definitions of class which focus on the technical and/or authority relations of production (Wright, 1980a and 1980b). This distinction is the source of the Marxist thesis that class relationships are inherently antagonistic and is at the core of all Wright's class maps.

However, in his fuller version of class map I and in his class map II, there are contradictory 'middle class' locations, the identification of which depends upon an analysis of the occupational hierarchy. As we have seen, initially Wright defines these non-working class employees in terms of different degrees of control over money, i.e. investment, the physical means of production, i.e. work, and labour-power, i.e. people. Thus, Wright is fully aware that relations of control play a part in his definition of these intermediate class positions, but considers them to be of secondary, not primary, importance. At the very least therefore, occupational considerations are not excluded from Wright's class analysis from the beginning.

To what extent does the move to an exploitation-centred conception of class overcome this problem? Wright claims that organizational and skill/credential assets are forms of exploitation, albeit secondary ones, and also the basis of antagonistic class relations. Conversely, it could be argued that these assets are not separate and therefore the basis of distinctive forms of exploitation, but are occupational characteristics. For example, Carchedi has argued that: 'The separation between the ownership of capital assets and ownership of organization assets is meaningless since to control the organization of capital assets is to own them, in the effective, economic sense' (1989: 110). It has also been noted that skilled and credentialized workers cooperate with other propertyless workers for the benefit of 'the capitalist exploiter' (Stinchcombe 1989: 177). These points raise serious doubts about Wright's theory of multiple exploitations and multiple class locations. Thus, the unequal distribution of organization and skill/credential assets is not the basis of exploitative class relations, but relates to differences in the technical division of labour or authority relations within the propertyless class(es).

Therefore in terms of Wright's own characterization of Marxist class theory, neither of his two class maps are purely Marxist since they contain gradational as well as relational elements. There is also the problem of his selection of key features. It could be argued that the theories of surplus value and proletarian revolutionary change are also crucial to Marxism, and although he is aware of their centrality to the Marxian theory of class, he fails to include them in his list of defining features. Perhaps this is because he considers that in advanced capitalism the 'middle class' has 'the potential to pose an alternative to capitalism' (Wright 1985: 89).

GOLDTHORPE'S NEO-WEBERIAN THEORY OF CLASS

Goldthorpe has been analysing the British class structure since the 1960s (Goldthorpe and Lockwood 1963). His early empirical research with Lockwood and others was predicated on the distinction between the manual working classes and the non-manual middle classes, and drew upon an occupational status scale that was widely used at the time (Goldthorpe *et al.* 1968 and 1969). The modified version of the Hall-Jones scale that was used in the *Affluent Worker* project can be compared to the class scheme that was developed by Goldthorpe in his later empirical research known as thc Oxford study of (malc) social mobility (1987). Both class maps include a matching range of class categories that are put into three similarly labelled groupings; white-collar/service classes, intermediate classes and manual/working classes (Goldthorpe *et al.* 1969: 197; Goldthorpe 1987: 40–3).

Goldthorpe's widely used sevenfold class scheme was constructed by 'aggregating categories from the collapsed (36-category) version of the Hope-Goldthorpe occupational scale' (Goldthorpe 1987: 40; see also Goldthorpe and Hope 1974). The aggregation of categories of this scale 'was carried out without reference to the position of the categories in the ordering of the scale', and that consequently, this class scheme is not 'consistently hierarchical' (Goldthorpe 1987: 43). Goldthorpe has also emphasized that these class categories are quite distinctive in the sense that 'they provide a relatively high degree of differentiation in terms of both occupational function and employment status: in effect, the associated employment status is treated as part of the definition of an occupation' (1987: 40). The justification for constructing a class scheme which incorporates both the technical relations of production and the social relations of production is that within the classes distinguished, it brings together 'occupations whose incumbents will typically share in broadly similar market and work situations' (1987: 40). Thus:

> We combine occupational categories whose members would appear in the light of available evidence, to be typically, comparable, on the one hand, in terms of their

> sources and levels of income, their degree of economic security and chances of economic advancement [i.e. market situation]; and on the other, in their location within the systems of authority and control governing the process of production in which they are engaged [i.e. work situation].
>
> (Goldthorpe *et al.* 1987: 40)

Beyond these important points of clarification, in marked contrast to Wright, Goldthorpe introduced his class scheme with the minimum of explanation. However, the neo-Weberian pedigree of this class scheme is readily apparent from his attempt to combine within a single model Weber's two basic class elements: the possession of property for exchange and marketable knowledge/skills. This was acknowledged explicitly by Goldthorpe in a separate publication (Goldthorpe and Bevan 1977: 280–1), and has been noted by others (e.g. Marshall *et al.* 1988: 21). The theoretical conduit that links Goldthorpe to Weber is of course Lockwood's distinction between work and market situations (Lockwood 1958). Echoing Lockwood, Goldthorpe claimed that these dimensions are 'the two main components of class position' (1987: 40).

Figure 2.4 Goldthorpe's class scheme (original version)

  I Higher-grade professionals, self-employed or salaried; higher-grade administrators and officials; managers in large industrial establishments; and large proprietors

 II Lower-grade professionals and higher-grade technicians; lower-grade administrators and officials; managers in small business and industrial establishments and in services; and supervisors of non-manual employees

III Routine non-manual employees in administration and commerce; sales personnel; and other rank-and-file employees in services

IV Small proprietors; self-employed artisans; and other own account workers apart from professionals

 V Lower-grade technicians; supervisors of manual workers

VI Skilled manual wage-workers in all branches of industry

VII Semi and unskilled manual workers; and agricultural workers

Notes: Classes I & II = Service Class
Classes III, IV & V = Intermediate Class
Classes VI & VII = Working Class
Source: Goldthorpe 1987: 40–3

Thus, the key assumption behind the three class groupings is that they contain classes that are regarded as comparable in terms of their work and market situations. The service class includes both propertied and propertyless classes but only white-collar occupations, and is thought to be more prestigious than all the other classes. The intermediate class is mixed in two respects; it includes both propertied and propertyless classes, plus blue- and white-collar occupations. The working class is the only 'pure' class in that it includes only propertyless manual workers. Consequently, the service and intermediate classes contain both relational and gradational elements. This class scheme was used by Goldthorpe and his research associates to study the social mobility of men in England and Wales (typically referred to as Britain).

Figure 2.5 Goldthorpe's class scheme (revised version)

1 *Classes I and II* All professionals, administrators and managers (including large proprietors), higher-grade technicians and supervisors of non-manual workers
2 *Class III* Routine non-manual employees in administration and commerce, sales personnel, other rank-and-file service workers
3 *Class IVab* Small proprietors, self-employed artisans and other 'own-account' workers with and without employees (other than in primary production)[a]
4 *Class IVc* Farmers and smallholders and other self-employed workers in primary production
5 *Classes V and VI* Lower-grade technicians; supervisors of manual workers and skilled manual workers
6 *Class VIIa* Semi- and unskilled manual workers (other than in primary production)
7 *Class VIIb* Agricultural and other workers in primary production[b]

Notes: (a) Where possible, those with and without employees are differentiated as IVa and IVb respectively. (b) The 'labelling of classes by combinations of roman numerals and letters' is Goldthorpian (Erikson and Goldthorpe 1992: 37).
Classes I & II = Service Class (i.e. 1)
Classes III, IVab & IVc = Intermediate Class (i.e. 2, 3 & 4)
Classes V & VI, VIIa & VIIb = Working Class (i.e. 5, 6 & 7)
Source: Goldthorpe 1987: 305

It was revised for the purpose of cross-national (male) mobility research but remained a seven-class scheme (Erikson, Goldthorpe and Portocarero 1979). The main changes involved the merging of the two service classes, namely classes I and II in the original scheme, and classes V and VI due to the 'difficulties in making the divisions between them in a cross-nationally consistent way' (Goldthorpe 1987: 304). It was also considered 'possible, and for comparative purposes highly desirable, to separate out within Classes IV and VII their agricultural components – that is, to distinguish a class of farmers, Class IVc and a class of agricultural workers, Class VIIb' (Goldthorpe 1987: 305).

The most confusing revision is arguably the merging of classes V and VI in an expanded 'working class', since in the original scheme the former class of lower-grade technicians and supervisors of manual workers is described as 'intermediate' on the basis of their structural location 'between the service class and the working class' (Goldthorpe 1987: 42). The use of the term 'blue-collar classes' in addition to the category working class would seem to indicate an awareness of this problem, although no discussion is forthcoming beyond noting at the outset that this 'blue-collar elite' is a marginal class (Goldthorpe 1987: 309 and 42). In the most recent and fullest account of Goldthorpe's approach to class, the 'problematic' class character of lower-grade technicians and supervisors of manual workers is reiterated but unresolved (Erikson and Goldthorpe 1992: 44). On the one hand they are regarded as part of the intermediate class in recognition of their authority and staff status, and on the other hand, as part of the 'skilled workers' element of the working class due to their relatively limited promotion prospects and the manual character of some of their work. At the very least, Goldthorpe's class of lower-grade technicians and supervisors of manual workers is less than homogeneous and hence raises doubts about the usefulness of the manual/non-manual distinction that is crucial to the three-class version of his class schema (Ahrne 1990; Penn 1981). This point relates to the criticisms of Goldthorpe's approach to class which is the focus of the next section.

A CRITIQUE OF GOLDTHORPE

Goldthorpe's early class analysis utilized an occupational scale that was organized around the distinction between a non-manual middle class and a manual working class. This approach to the 'class' structure has been the subject of considerable critical attention and will be commented upon in the next section. This critique focuses on the two seven-class versions outlined above, both of which were constructed on neo-Weberian principles, and anticipates some of the material discussed in the next chapter. Thus, although the original and revised versions were developed to deal with different research objectives, namely, national (England) and cross-national (England, France and Sweden) mobility research respectively, they are systematically related and therefore comparable.

The first criticism of Goldthorpe's efforts to conceptualize the class structure of advanced capitalist societies concerns his use of relational and gradational dimensions within one class scheme amd within class groupings. According to Ossowski (1969), a relational definition of class typically involves an essentially dichotomous structure charcacterized by two diametrically opposed classes, the relationship between them being one of advantage at the expense of the other. By contrast, a gradational definition of class typically involves, at the very minimum, a trichotomous structure characterized by many divisions, each of which is considered higher or lower than the others in one or more respects. The Marxian theory of exploitative class relations affords a familiar and excellent example of the former, whereas occupational class/status models based on a hierarchy of skill and or prestige are examples of the latter (see following section). Like Wright's revised scheme, i.e. class map II, Goldthorpe's approach to class appears to contain elements of both within the same model, though it tends to give priority to gradational rather than relational factors and is described for the most part in the language of hierarchy (Ahrne 1990).

A second and related issue concerns Goldthorpe's use of the term service class. This term was introduced in the 1950s by the neo-Marxist sociologist Renner (1978) and developed by the neo-Weberian sociologist Dahrendorf (1964) to refer to those in the middle of the class structure who manage private or public capital. Abercrombie and Urry have pointed out that Goldthorpe's idea of a service class is very different from the earlier formulation:

> First, it is an aggregation of occupations rather than a class united by the performance of services for a capitalist

or within a bureaucracy. Secondly, it is not an intermediate class but is rather at the top of the hierarchy.

(1983: 32)

Thus, Goldthorpe has effectively enhanced the significance of the service class at the expense of the capitalist class. Merging service-class workers with large proprietors implies that these two classes are equal in certain respects, such as income and power, thereby undermining the distinctiveness of both (Penn 1981; Savage *et al.* 1992). The claim that professional and managerial workers at the apex of private and public bureaucracies are indistinguishable from the owners of capital can be challenged on the grounds that 'a decline in personal forms of control does not necessarily spell the decline of the capitalist class itself' (Scott 1991: 65; see also Bottomore and Brym 1989). As noted by Scott, the service class 'serve' capital and hence capitalists.

Third, and following from both the above points, assigning routine white-collar employees and small proprietors to a broad class labelled 'intermediate', is contradictory and confusing (Penn 1981). The main reasons for this are that compared to many public sector bureaucratic employees, some small proprietors are in a very precarious class situation. On the other hand, compared to many private sector bureaucratic employees, some small proprietors may be in a very advantageous class situation. Finally, in a society dominated by capitalist values there would seem to be an argument for ranking entrepreneurs above employees, other things being equal.

Fourth, Goldthorpe's approach to class has been the subject of an extensive 'feminist critique' (Abbott and Wallace 1990), with particular reference to the male head of household unit of class analysis and his tendency to concentrate, especially in his earlier mobility research, his degree of coverage on males.

More specifically, it has been noted that since there are important differences in the work and market situations of women in routine non-manual jobs 'the Goldthorpe classes need to be revised for use with women's occupations' (Heath and Britten 1984: 489). In fact Goldthorpe concedes this point by dividing class III into two classes, IIIa and IIIb, and then combining class IIIb with (working) class VII 'in order to make the schema more suited to the class allocation of women' (Goldthorpe 1987: 279). However, others consider that this revision does not go far enough to take into account the distinctiveness of women's class situation and have therefore devised alternative class schemes (Murgatroyd 1982; Dale *et al.* 1985; see also Abbott and Sapsford 1987).

Finally, in the most recent account of Goldthorpe's class scheme it is claimed that it is derived from the classic contributions of Weber and Marx. Starting from the Marxian and Weberian assumption that employment relations are central to class, 'a basic threefold division of class positions' is outlined; employers, self-employed workers and employees, and developed into the five, seven and elevenfold versions of this class scheme (Erikson and Goldthorpe 1992: 37). In the expanded versions, the alleged Marxist error of not recognizing the increased heterogeneity of the employee class is avoided by distinguishing between different categories of service and between intermediate and non-manual workers, although the problem of homogeneity remains, especially in the service class.

A NOTE ON OCCUPATIONAL CLASS (STATUS)

There is one other approach to class that is widely used in sociological research in Britain and America, and that is to define class in occupational status terms. The tendency to call the occupational status categories used in these schemes classes is potentially very confusing and arguably reflects the complexity and uncertainty that surrounds the relationship between class and status (cf. Abercrombie and Urry 1983; Duke and Edgell 1987; Giddens 1979: Lockwood 1958). It may also be indicative of a reluctance to use the controversial and highly politicized term class that is associated indelibly with Marx, and of a preference for the Weberian idea of status which, it is thought, can be more easily achieved via a change in one's pattern of consumption and lifestyle. In the interests of clarity, in this study the term social class will be used to refer to social relations of production (i.e. employment relations), such as those advocated by Wright in his early studies (e.g. 1976 and 1979). The term occupational class will be reserved for schemes that are based on one or other features of occupations, for example prestige or skill, such as those developed by British and American Census statisticians (Conk 1978; Hodge *et al.* 1967; Leete and Fox 1977; Reid 1989). Since these are government inspired classifications, they are often called official class schemes (Nichols 1979; Marshall 1988).

A good example of this approach to 'class' is the occupational status scale that has been developed in Britain this century by the Registrar General. Since the 1911 census the Registrar General has classified occupations on the basis of their standing in the community and allocated them to five broad categories known as 'social classes'. Up to the 1971 census the main 'classes' were listed as in Figure 2.6.

Figure 2.6 The Registrar General's 'social classes'

1 Professional occupations
2 Intermediate occupations
3 Skilled occupations
4 Partly skilled occupations
5 Unskilled occupations

Source: Leete and Fox 1977: 2

The occupations in classes 1 and 2 are usually regarded as non-manual and those in classes 4 and 5 as manual, and due to its size and mixed character class 3 was often split by social researchers into 3N (non-manual) and 3M (manual). This convention was adopted as a standard procedure in the 1970 Classification of Occupations (Leete and Fox 1977). Thus the scheme is essentially an occupational status hierarchy that implies that the major social division in society is between those engaged in manual and non-manual work.

In 1980 over fifty years of tradition were abandoned when the Registrar General redefined 'social class' as occupational skill rather than as occupational prestige (OPCS 1980). However, this change was more apparent than real, in that the classes remained the same in the hope that comparability would be preserved (Boston 1980; Brewer 1986). Thus, although the 1970 and 1980 official class schemes contrast conceptually, 'they do not show any important differences in their empirical relations with a variety of social, educational and health variables' (Brewer 1986: 131) In Britain the Registrar General's occupational approach to class dominates official statistics and until recently also dominated empirical research (Nichols 1979; Duke and Edgell 1987).

The main assumption behind occupational status scales is that occupation is the best single indicator of a person's social standing (Szreter 1984). Drudy (1991) has summarized the essentially pragmatic case for the continued use of this type of official occupational class scheme as follows:

1 that since it is a state scheme it enables researchers to compare their findings with official figures;
2 that it is easy to use in the sense that it only requires a simple job description, not detailed information, and is not difficult to interpret;
3 that it has been available for a long time, indeed is still used extensively by empirical social researchers and policy makers, hence it is appropriate for all kinds of comparative research.

However, it has been subject to an increasing barrage of criticisms for unlike the other two schemes discussed in this chapter, it is not theoretically informed by either Marxian or Weberian theory. Although its intellectual origins are empirical rather than theoretical (Szreter 1984), the assumption of shared values that is built into the idea that there exists a hierarchy of occupations that may be conceptualized on a status scale means that it can be located within the functionalist theoretical approach to social stratification (Tumin 1970; Drudy 1991). Even if one assumes that the same jobs enjoy the same prestige in all societies, many are demoted or promoted over time as a result of processes such as enskilling, deskilling and feminization (Davies 1980; Dex 1985). Moreover, the suggestion that official occupational classes are 'essentially descriptive categories that relate to status', means that such class schemes are 'consonant' with key elements in the dominant ideology (Nichols 1979: 165). Notable in this respect is the idea that modern capitalism is a unitary type of society characterized by individually achieved occupational mobility and without an identifiable capitalist class (Drudy 1991). Consequently, the official class scheme, and its associated managerialist ideology, tend to deny the existence of capitalists and the inherited nature of their privileges. Therefore, such a scheme can describe the class-related income inequalities but cannot explain the larger inequalities that arise from the ownership of capital.

It has also been shown to be unreliable due to problems that arise from coding its unclear and general categories (Leete and Fox 1977). Faulty classification is particularly acute in the middle of the hierarchy, where it is necessary to distinguish between skilled manual and non-manual occupations (Bland 1979). Moreover, the way in which occupations are allocated to a 'social class' leads to many anomalies, such as managers of a few workers ending up in the same class as managers of large organizations (Drudy 1991).

In addition to these theoretical and empirical criticisms, consideration of the history of the official occupational class scheme used in Britain during this century led to the conclusion that it is 'obsolete' and 'simplistic', in sum, a 'pseudo-analytical' conceptualization (Szreter 1984). The recent change in the occupational basis of the scheme from prestige to skill level has done little to alter this view, hence it remains 'an arbitrary and crude, but well used, measure of social inequality' (Brewer 1986: 139).

SUMMARY AND CONCLUSIONS

There has always been an overlap between the Marxian and Weberian conceptualizations of class. This was acknowledged by Weber with reference to the centrality of property to class analysis and to the greater importance of class situation compared to status situation. It was also confirmed by Lockwood's conclusion that ' "class" factors are of overriding importance' (1958: 212). Moreover, Goldthorpe and Lockwood have long held that: 'Weber's idea of "class situation" is very similar to that of Marx' (1963: 157). The recent attempts by Wright to build upon Marx's approach to class by introducing non-property based classes, and Goldthorpe's elaboration of Weber's approach to class on the basis of the distinction between work and market situations has, arguably, increased the convergence between them. More specifically, both Wright and Goldthorpe recognize that class advantages can derive from the ownership of property, the possession of knowledge and/or skills, and the possession of physical labour power, and that as a consequence, the class situations and class groupings that make up their respective class maps increasingly resemble each other. There is therefore an 'emerging consensus on what constitues a social class and . . . the general shape of current class arrangements' (Waters 1991: 163).

However, dissent from the hitherto conventional view that the Marxian and Weberian conceptions of class diverge, such as that expressed by Erikson and Goldthorpe (1992: 37), needs to be qualified in at least three interrelated respects. First, although the latest neo-Marxist and neo-Weberian approaches to class contain employment and occupational dimensions, the former are

essentially relational whereas the latter are essentially gradational. Second, neo-Marxists retain the idea of a distinctive
capitalist class but neo-Weberians tend to obscure the existence
of this small yet still powerful class. Finally, the main fault line
in the class structures of modern societies is between employers
and employees in Wright's neo-Marxist scheme, whereas in Goldthorpe's threefold version of his neo-Weberian scheme the main
division is between non-manual and manual workers. In sum, the
main advantage of neo-Marxist conceptions of class is that they
differentiate capitalists from non-capitalists, in contrast to neo
Weberian conceptions, whose main advantage is that they distinguish between a variety of non-capitalist classes. Conversely, the
main limitation of these respective approaches to class concern
the issue of the extent to which the classes identified are homogeneous. Thus, in the case of Wright's schemes it has been shown
that his conceptualization of the proletariat includes many routine
white-collar workers whose mobility chances, self-assigned class
and voting behaviour clearly differentiates them from the manual
working class (Marshall 1988; Marshall et al. 1988). Similarly, it
has been argued that Goldthorpe's definition of the service class
contains a wide range of class situations such as employers and
employees, as well as a diversity of non-manual classes (Savage
et al. 1992).

Occupational class schemes, on the other hand are explicitly
hierarchical and deny totally the existence of the capitalist class.
To the extent that occupations are a basic ingredient of all class
maps, the dynamic nature of occupations bedevils them all, but
is acute in the case of cross-national (ILO 1968) and historical
comparisons of class (Hakim 1980), and for models based exclusively on occupation (Duke and Edgell 1987).

The theoretical meaning of class is the first step in the process
of operationalizing this key, yet highly contested, sociological
concept.

3

The measurement of class

INTRODUCTION

The process by which the classical and contemporary approaches to the meaning of class discussed in the first two chapters are transformed from a theoretical idea into a measurable form is called operationalization. On the assumption that it is both desirable and possible to develop a 'scientific sociology', the process of operationalizing concepts is crucial to the achievement of reliable (i.e. the extent to which repeated measurements produce the same results under the same conditions) and valid (i.e. the extent to which a measure is an accurate representation of the phenomenon the researcher wishes to investigate) empirical data. Thus, operational definitions impart clarity and precision to sociological analysis and are therefore at the core of empirical sociology (cf. Pawson 1989). Since class is simultaneously one of the most important and widely used and abused concepts in sociology, in addition to being one of the most controversial, it is imperative to be clear from the outset not only what one means by the term, but also how one intends to measure it. Until recently, this aspect of class analysis had received little attention in contrast to the plethora of theoretical and substantive contributions. The change in emphasis has been stimulated by the reorientation of neo-Marxism away from abstract theorizing and toward empirical analysis (e.g. Wright 1979), and by the emergence of a feminist critique of 'malestream' sociology (Abbott and Wallace 1990).

A CRITIQUE OF THE TRADITIONAL ANALYTIC CLASS FRAMEWORK

In a recent review of how class was operationalized in contemporary British sociology it was found that the vast majority of studies defined class in occupational terms, concentrated on people who were economically active on a full-time basis, assumed that the family is the basic unit of class analysis, and that its class location is determined by the occupation of the male 'head' of the household (Duke and Edgell 1987; Edgell and Duke 1991). This approach to the measurement of class was called the traditional analytic class framework.

Four lines of overlapping criticism can be levelled at this framework: (1) empirical; (2) feminist; (3) sectoral and (4) neo-Marxist.

1 The major empirical objection to the traditional analytic class framework is that it leads to discussions of class based on unrepresentative samples. This is because at worst, focusing solely on economically active males excludes nearly two-thirds of the adult population in a society like Britain (Duke and Edgell 1987). The main social categories excluded by this approach include women, the retired, students, the unemployed and the underemployed. Although these groups are not mutually exclusive – for example, the vast majority of part-time workers are women – in a society characterized by increasing numbers of women workers, casual workers, retired workers, unemployed workers and students, the validity of generalizations based on research informed by the traditional analytic class framework are more questionable than ever.

2 Feminist criticisms of the traditional analytic class framework have been at the forefront of the sociological debate about how to operationalize class. As a consequence, the literature on the gender dimension of class measurement

is extensive and evident in a variety of academic journals over the past three decades (e.g. Watson and Barth 1964; Acker 1973; Heath and Britten 1984; Wright 1989), collections of articles (e.g. Gamarnikow *et al.* 1983; Crompton and Mann 1986), monographs (e.g. Abbott and Sapsford 1987; Edgell and Duke 1991), specialist textbooks (e.g. Dex 1985; Roberts 1981) and general textbooks (e.g. Abbott and Wallace 1990). The main thrust of the feminist critique is that to exclude women from class analysis on *a priori* grounds is both sexist and unsociological. It is sexist in the sense that to overlook women implies that this half of the population is of insufficient importance to be incorporated into class analysis. It is unsociological to the extent that by excluding women, in advance of ascertaining their relevance to a particular study of class, involves basing research on what may turn out to be wholly unwarranted assumptions. Social trends such as the tendency for increasing numbers of married women to work outside the home, and the growth of one-parent families, suggests that the force of the feminist critique of the traditional analytic class framework, which is renowned for concentrating on full-time economically active males and/or on male 'heads' of households, is also gaining strength on historical grounds. This is especially true for those cross-class families in which the wife is in a superior occupational class than her husband (McRae 1986).

3 Sectoral criticisms of the traditional analytic class framework concern the extent to which the division of the employed population into public and private sector workers can be incorporated neatly into any one class scheme. In view of the growth of the state sector in America, Britain and continental Europe during the twentieth century (O'Connor 1973), it is important not to overlook this social division in class analysis. In fact, in Britain over the past decade or so the division between highly unionized public employees and lowly unionized private employees is thought to have become more important politically as the public sector has been reduced and the private sector expanded (Dunleavy 1980; Dunleavy and Husbands 1985; Edgell and Duke 1983 and 1991). Consequently, there is a strong case for adopting a class scheme that is compatible with production sectoral analysis. In terms of the basic

choice between social, occupational and mixed class schemes, the first type of class scheme fits best with production sector categories. This is because in a social class scheme, large and small employers are automatically classified as self-employed, and only the employee categories are divided into public or private sectors. It has been shown that the ability to accommodate both class and production sector effects into the same model is an advantage in class analysis (Edgell and Duke 1986). Moreover, the suggestion that the manual/non-manual distinction should be retained in class analysis (Marshall 1988), despite inconsistent interpretations (Erikson and Goldthorpe 1992), can be heeded by dividing employees in this way (Dunleavy and Husbands 1985).

4 Neo-Marxist criticisms were discussed above in the context of the work of Goldthorpe (see Chapter 2), therefore a brief recapitulation and explication with reference to the traditional analytic class framework will suffice. To the extent that this approach to the measurement of class involves occupational rather than social class, the neo-Marxist capitalist society argument that gradational class schemes obscure the most powerful and distinctive capitalist (i.e. employer) class can be extended to claim that pure occupational class measures render this key class invisible. In other words, it is not simply a matter of conflating the property and non-property (e.g. organizational and/or skill assets) bases of class, as in the case of a mixed scheme like Goldthorpe's, but constructing a class scheme that ignores the ownership of the means of production dimension altogether. By implication, the manual/non-manual dichotomy inherent in the traditional analytic class framework is flawed on the grounds that it fails to reflect what is arguably the most significant social cleavage in a capitalist society, namely the conflict of interests between the owners and non-owners of capital. After all, it is not just manual workers who are vulnerable to the vicissitudes of a market system. Another neo-Marxist criticism concerns the susceptibility of occupationally-based measures of class to changes in the occupational structure associated with the twin processes of deskilling and enskilling (Duke and Edgell 1987). Such changes make it imperative to review the relative position of all jobs that have been affected by these social

processes, which in turn complicates any attempt to generalize historically.

In sum, the first two lines of criticism of the traditional analytic class framework – the empirical and the feminist – focus on the issue of to whom to apply one's class scheme, whereas the third and fourth critiques – the sectoral and the neo-Marxist – concern the theoretical/conceptual basis of class. These criticisms apply to a greater or lesser extent to both neo-Marxist and neo-Weberian studies of class. For example, Wright admits without explanation that in his book on the American and Swedish class structures he 'will only analyse the working labour force' (1985: 160). Goldthorpe on the other hand, in the face a wide-ranging, but often misdirected attack on his view, has defended stoutly his claim that in the study of class mobility

> the class position of the family is a unitary one which derives from that of its male 'head' – in the sense of the family member who has the fullest commitment to labour-market participation.
>
> (Goldthorpe 1984: 492)

CLASS OPERATIONALIZATION: THE THREE KEY CHOICES

Dissatisfaction with the traditional analytic class framework has led to the view that in order to systematically and comprehensively translate the abstract idea of class into a measureable concept, social researchers need to make three interrelated choices (Duke and Edgell 1987; Edgell and Duke 1991). The first choice, discussed already in Chapters 1 and 2, involves which conceptual scheme to use, i.e. a social class scheme, an occupational class scheme, or a mixed one, and, by implication, which theory of class to draw upon, i.e. neo-Marxist theory, neo-Weberian theory, or both. The second and third choices concern to whom the selected class categories should be applied. This involves two distinct yet linked decisions. First, should the unit of class analysis be the respondent/individual or the family/household? Second, should the degree of coverage of the population be all adult respondents/household members or only the economically active respondents/household members?

These three choices have not received equal attention from

sociologists. Conceptual and gender issues have tended to dominate the literature in the recent past, the degree of coverage is hardly ever discussed, and it is rare for all three choices to be considered together.

Choice one: conceptual scheme

Since the choice of which conceptual scheme to adopt has been discussed above, the purpose of this summary is to outline the main options and their implications, both theoretical and empirical.

In the light of the above discussion about the meaning of class, the conceptual scheme decision can be reduced to three basic options: (a) occupational class; (b) social class; and (c) occupational and social class.

Occupational class schemes such as the Registrar General's are organized exclusively with reference to the technical relations of production. They consequently give primacy to the manual/non-manual boundary, which is often referred to as the blue/white-collar division in the sociology of work and as the working/middle-class division in the sociology of social stratification. Typically, pure occupational class schemes are subdivided according to varying skill and/or status levels within each main category. In addition to dominating official statistics and empirical social research in Britain, occupational class schemes also tend to dominate everyday discourse in that the two most frequently mentioned categories are the 'middle' and 'working' classes (Coxon *et al.* 1986). To recap from the previous chapter, occupational class schemes are gradational and therefore tend to emphasize the consensual, fragmented and open nature of class structures.

The main limitations of occupational class schemes concern the salience of the manual/non-manual dichotomy primarily because it fails to recognize the centrality of property ownership, its vulnerability to changes in the occupational structure, and the claim that it is contaminated by gender (Duke and Edgell 1987). On the plus side is the assertion that occuaptional class schemes are useful in predictive terms, although this is a weak argument given the availability of more theoretically informed and carefully constructed alternatives (Marshall *et al.* 1988). However, they are widely used and hence facilitate replication and comparability, which may be important considerations, especially in many small-scale research projects.

Social class schemes such as the early versions of Wright are organized solely with reference to the social relations of production. They therefore highlight the ownership/non-ownership division and are usually subdivided into large and small employers, and managerial and non-managerial employees. As already noted, such schemes are relational rather than gradational and consequently tend to emphasize the conflictual, polarized and closed character of class structures.

In addition to Wright's autocritique of his first class map, and neo-Weberian criticisms of it concerning the lack of homogeneity of some of his class categories (see Chapter 2), a more general theoretical objection to Wright's original scheme is that, like all neo-Marxist structuralist accounts of class, it is 'static, mechanical, crudely deterministic and . . . devoid of human agency' (Marshall et al. 1988: 24). It has also been argued that such schemes inflate the size of the capitalist class (Marsh 1986). Moreover, arguably, since large-scale owners tend to be involved in management and managers often have a share in ownership, these two class categories should be merged (Erikson and Goldthorpe 1992). At the same time it has been claimed that 'it is the incoherence of Wright's empirical findings that casts serious doubts on the utility of his approach' (Marshall et al. 1988: 265). In other words, in practice Wright's original scheme works less well than Goldthorpe's neo-Weberian alternative. However, it has been pointed out that Wright's first scheme is more thoroughly Marxist in the sense that it excludes occupational elements (Marshall 1988), and that it has been successfully used in America (e.g. Wright 1979) and Britain (Edgell and Duke 1991).

It has been noted above (see Chapter 2) that Wright's revisions to his first class map moved it in a neo-Weberian direction. In fact, it has been argued that Wright 'has effectively rejected a wholly structural account of class' in favour of a more dynamic 'trajectory' approach (Marshall et al. 1988: 43–4). Consequently, Wright's transformed second class map has been criticized for being 'non-Marxist'! (Marshall et al., 1988: 47). Alternatively it could be argued that it is less strictly, though still essentially, Marxist since it is founded upon Marx's fundamental class division between the owners and non-owners of capital. Labels aside, the introduction of the Weberian dimensions of organization assets and skill assets into Wright's class map II has led to a number of criticisms. First, that it is not easy to 'separate the two assets in most contexts', and second, that unlike property, and to a lesser extent skills, organization assets 'cannot be stored outside the organizational context' (Savage *et al*. 1992: 15). Moreover, the idea of skill assets is regarded as especially problematic because it is unclear 'how a person with skill assets exploits the unskilled' (Savage *et al*. 1992: 15).

A general point that applies to all relational conceptualizations of class is that they are not easily converted into a hierarchy, although given the practical and ideological importance of private property in a capitalist society, it could be argued that propertied classes should be ranked higher than propertyless classes (Edgell and Duke 1991).

In view of the points advanced in the above critique of the traditional analytic class framework, the main advantages of a social class scheme can be summarized as follows. First and most important of all, social class schemes give due recognition to the key economic and political significance of the capitalist class and their relationship to non-capitalist classes, although this class may be very small and difficult to identify in empirical research. Second, the relational dimension of social class schemes provides them with a dynamism that is crucial to the explanation of inequalities, including the role of social formations in the distribution of wealth and power. Third, social class schemes are less vulnerable than pure occupational ones to changes in the occupational structure, and they also tend to be less contaminated by gender and occupation. Fourth, the problem of a lack of class homogeneity can be overcome with ease by subdividing the non-propertied classes by type of work (e.g. manual and non-manual) or by sector (e.g. public or private).

Class schemes that combine occupational and social class, such as Wright's second class map and Goldthorpe's schema, raise the question of the extent to which it is possible to incorporate gradational and relational class in the one model. More specifically, it could be argued that the organizing principles that inform occupational and social class schemes are basically incompatible. For example, occupational class implies shared values, whereas social class implies conflicting interests. Moreover, unlike the two 'pure' schemes, mixed schemes typically include both social and occupational classes, although they tend to give primacy to one or the other. Such schemes also tend to be trichotomous in that the various categories can be collapsed into three main class groupings: the capitalist or service class, the intermediate classes and the working classes (Goldthorpe 1987: 70). However, if a mixed scheme is expressed in the language of hierarchy and places non-propertied classes equal top of the class structure, such schemes are essentially gradational and therefore implicitly occupational rather than social relational. It is stretching socio-logical credibility to locate university lecturers in the same class as the owners of large capital.

On the other hand it could be argued that since industrial capitalist societies are neither totally harmonious nor totally con-flict ridden, class schemes based solely on one of these two assumptions are unrealistic. In other words, class structures reflect shared values and conlicting interests. Thus, what is required is a class scheme which taps these two dimensions of a modern social structure. Whether or not any one scheme does so successfully or at all is a matter of both theoretical and empirical judgement (Pawson 1989), although it has been claimed that 'it is consequences, not antecedents, that matter' (Erikson and Goldthorpe 1992: 37). What is clear is that no one scheme has a monopoly of advantages or disadvantages, and that much depends upon one's research aims.

Choice two: unit of analysis

Having selected a conceptual scheme to use in one's class analy-sis, the next step is to decide to whom to apply the class categor-ies: the respondent/individual or the family/household?

Those who research class within the traditional analytic frame-work tend to apply their occupational class categories to the family/household and treat the 'male' as the head of the house-hold. As noted above, the case for this approach to the unit of analysis choice has been advocated forcibly by Goldthorpe (1983; 1984). He claims that family members share the same class posi-tion and that this is best measured by the male head because he is usually 'the family member who has the greatest commitment to, and continuity in, labour market participation' (Goldthorpe 1983: 470). The first part of Goldthorpe's argument, that when couples live together they form a household and share similar, but not necessarily equal, material conditions and life-chances, has been criticized (e.g. Walby 1986; Wright 1989), albeit mistakenly according to Goldthorpe (cf. Erikson and Goldthorpe 1992), but is far less contentious than the second part concerning how best to measure a family's class. Goldthorpe claims that despite the increase in the employment of married women (cf. Reid and Wormald 1982), 'the husband's employment remains the dominant factor' (Goldthorpe 1983: 469). This is because married women are still constrained in their labour market participation by their family and domestic responsibilities (cf. Edgell 1980; Finch 1983). To paraphrase Giddens (1979), and Heath and Britten (1984), women have experienced more liberation outside the home than inside it, but not enough to make a difference. Hence, married women remain, to a greater or lesser extent, dependent upon their husbands. Thus, a family's class position is still determined by that of the 'head' who is usually a male. Goldthorpe notes that the main exception to this rule is a cross-class family where the 'wife's type of employment is not only different from, but also superior to that of her husband' (1983: 479). However, in Goldthorpe's view, once spurious cross-class families are discounted (e.g. routine non-manual occupation wife and a manual occcupation husband), genuine cross-class families (e.g. service class wife and a worker husband) are so rare (cf. McRae 1986) that they pose no real threat to his position, notwithstanding claims to the contrary (e.g. Britten and Heath 1983).

A lively and at times acrimonious debate ensued concerning the unit of analysis following Goldthorpe's defence of the conventional male 'head' of household view (in addition to the references cited already, see Stanworth 1984; Goldthorpe 1984). In the process, Goldthorpe demonstrated that the apparently 'illogical' strategy, as Delphy (1981) has called it, of treating single and married women differently in class analysis, was neither illogical nor sexist (Goldthorpe and Payne 1986). However, as Dex has pointed out, 'Goldthorpe has clearly adapted, and in some respects changed, his position' (1990: 137). Specifically, Goldthorpe moved from his initial male 'head' of household approach to favouring the 'dominance' method for establishing a family's class, which, following Erikson (1984), involves consideration of 'the position of the family member who has, in some sense, the highest level of labour-market participation' (Goldthorpe 1984: 497). Thus, Goldthorpe still advocates a family/household unit of analysis but his approach to its determination is less androcentric (Erikson and Goldthorpe 1992).

Although the dominance approach overcomes the male 'head' of household problem, it requires a hierarchical class scheme with a clear order of dominance. In the case of relational schemes, it is considered appropriate for self-employment to take precedence (Erikson 1984). Finally, since the dominance principle tends to be applied upwards rather than downwards, it has the empirical effect of reducing the size of the 'lower' classes and expanding the size of the 'higher' classes (Edgell and Duke 1991).

The opposite of a group unit of class analysis is an individual one. The case for a respondent/individual indicator is that respondent attitudes and behaviour should logically be analysed in terms of the direct experience of the respondent. Hence, in the context of the debate about women and class analysis, Stanworth has argued that the direct employment of married women should not be disregarded since to do so 'implies' that this experience adds 'nothing to our understanding of class formation, class inequality and class action' (1984: 162). This approach has been contested by Goldthorpe, as noted above, who has argued that couples will share, to varying degrees, similar material conditions and class 'fate' (Erikson and Goldthorpe 1992: 233).

Alternatively, it could be argued that both the respondent and the family units of analysis are valid measures of class, it all depends on the research context (Edgell and Duke 1991). For example, in studies of production-related behaviour and attitudes, where the direct experience of the respondent is relevant, the focus should be on men and women as individuals. On the other hand, in research into consumption behaviour and attitudes, where the family as a whole consumes together to a greater or lesser extent, the appropriate unit of analysis is the family.

If the research context is deemed to require a group rather than an individual measure of class, the problem then becomes a matter of how best to measure class at this level. In the case of one-adult households, it is not a problem as the procedure is identical to using a respondent-based unit of analysis. However, in households containing two or more adults it is a potential problem because the adults concerned may not be in the same class. In this event, in addition to the two basic solutions considered so far, the male 'head' of household and the dominance method, there are two other more radical approaches; joint classifications and separate class schemes for men and women. Joint classifications, such as the one advanced by Britten and Heath (1983), are problematic due to the instability of women's labour market situation (Goldthorpe 1984). According to Goldthorpe, this produces 'rates of class mobility which are spuriously high – and which would thus defeat the purposes of class analysis'

(Goldthorpe 1984: 495; see also Erikson and Goldthorpe 1992: 238). The separate class schemes alternative, such as the Women's Social Groups classification advanced by Murgatroyd (1982 and 1984), is predicated in part on a critique of schemes that are developed for men and applied to women, for instance the Goldthorpe schema, and relatedly, in part on the extensive gender segregation that characterizes employment (Arber *et al*. 1986). For example, one of the most distinctive features of female employment is that much of it is part-time and often combined in the case of married women with the unpaid role of housewife. This is a problem for all schemes and relates to the third and final choice involved in operationalizing class, namely the degree of coverage decision.

Choice three: degree of coverage

The final key choice in the operationalization of class concerns the degree of coverage. Traditionally, only those adults who are economically active on a full-time basis are included in class analysis. This implies that all those who do not work full-time, the unemployed, part-time workers, the retired, and so on, are no longer part of the class structure. High levels of unemployment and underemployment, and hence the persistence of an under-class in contemporary industrial capitalist societies such as Britain and America (see Chapter 4), arguably strengthen the argument that all adults should be included in class analysis.

In empirical terms this choice is complicated by the various sociological meanings that can be attached to the notion of economic activity/inactivity. Thus, economic activity can range from workaholics, to casual workers, to those who are inactive on a permanent basis. In others words, there is regular and irregular full and part-time work outside the home in the formal sector of the economy, and there is informal 'off the books' work, voluntary work, and paid and unpaid work inside the home. Typically, class analysis only concerns itself with those active in the formal sector, yet the class structure of 'work' in the informal sector parallels the class structure of 'work' in the formal sector (Mattera 1985; Edgell and Hart 1988). Interestingly, the exclusion of unpaid housework from the official definition of economic activity dates from the 1881 Census in Britain (Hakim 1980).

It has been noted by Marshall *et al*. (1988) that one of the points of convergence between Wright's neo-Marxist and

Goldthorpe's neo-Weberian approach to class is that they both concentrate on those individuals who are in the official labour force on the grounds that they can be allocated directly and easily to a class. However, there would seem to be no more good reason for excluding the 'working unemployed' (Henry 1982) from class analysis than there is for excluding members of the leisure class who live off unearned income, such as absentee owners, or members of the vicarious leisure class, i.e. full-time housewives (Veblen 1970). This is the view taken by Erikson, who has asserted that: 'all of us have a class position, regardless of whether we participate in the labour force or not' (1984: 502). In view of the distinction between those who have a full-time job in the formal sector (active) and those who do not (inactive), if one wishes to include the latter category in class research, this can be achieved by reference to their most recent direct class experience or main previous direct class experience. This method is applicable to all those who have worked in the past, the vast majority, but not to those who have never worked, such as students. The inclusion of the economically 'inactive' in class analysis ensures that the sociological significance of this increasingly large and heterogeneous social category is not ruled out in advance of undertaking research on class.

SUMMARY AND CONCLUSIONS

The various ways of operationalizing class have different sociological implications, and some of these are illustrated in Table

Table 3.1 The effect of alternative operationalizations of class on the size of the working class and the proportion of the sample unclassified

Unit of analysis	Degree of coverage	Conceptual scheme	% Working class	% Unclassified
Respondent	EA only	OC	24	45
Respondent	EA only	SC	39	45
Respondent	All	OC	45	5
Respondent	All	SC	71	5
Household	EA only	OC	24	34
Household	EA only	SC	39	34
Household	All	OC	35	3
Household	All	SC	60	3

Source: Edgell and Duke 1991: 39

3.1 with special reference to the size of the working class and the unclassified population.

Table 3.1 shows that the size of the working class can vary enormously depending upon how it is defined in terms of the three key choices: conceptual scheme, unit of analysis and degree of coverage. For example, an exclusive focus on respondents who are economically active (EA) reduces the size of the working class and the comprehensiveness of the data.

In conclusion, different ways of operationalizing class produce quite different models of the class structure and much depends upon the sociological issues under investigation. Thus, if the research focus is production behaviour and attitudes, any conceptual scheme can be used but the unit of analysis should be the respondent and only the economically active should be included. Conversely, in a study of the social and political effects of Thatcherism, it was argued that both the economically inactive and active should be included using a household measure of social class (Edgell and Duke 1991). In actual research situations, in contrast to academic discussions of research methods, it may well be that considerations of cost and ease of data collection, coding and analysis, influence the decision of how to operationalize the concept class. For example, collecting sufficient information on all adult members of a household increases research costs (Duke and Edgell 1987), and the male 'head' of household method is far less complicated than joint measures of class position (Savage et al. 1992).

In the light of the complexity of the operational choices facing an empirical class researcher and the bewildering range of class situations and groupings that have been identified by social theorists of every hue, is it possible to answer the question: how many classes are there in modern industrial capitalist society? (Runciman 1990). Even specialists in the sociology of class seem uncertain. For instance, in Chapter 2 it was noted that Wright has suggested between two and twelve classes and Goldthorpe between three and thirty-six. According to Erikson and Goldthorpe, 'the only sensible' response to the number of classes issue is: 'As many as it proves empirically useful to distinguish for the analytical purposes at hand' (1992: 46). On the other hand, the number of classes identified will vary depending upon the historical and political circumstances. For example, the more fragmented and fluid the class structure, the greater the number of classes, whereas polarized two-class models emphasize the importance of class conflict (Ossowski 1969). Hence, although there is no definitive answer to this question, in the light of the increasing convergence of neo-Marxist and neo-Weberian class maps discussed above (see especially Chapter 2), for pedagogic purposes it is possible to reduce the great variety of class situations to three basic groupings with reference to the main sources of class power: property, knowledge and physical labour. However, as will become apparent in the next chapter, the exact constellation of class situations that comprise the main social classes and their designation is a matter of considerable debate.

4

Class structure and social change

INTRODUCTION

Thus far, the discussion has concentrated on the meaning of class in classical and contemporary Marxian and Weberian social theory plus the measurement of class. The purpose of this chapter is to consider the main classes in advanced capitalism with special reference to changes in America and Britain during this century. Notwithstanding the differences between Marx and Weber, notably with respect to the dynamics and future of class society, the class models developed by neo-Marxist and neo-Weberian theorists look increasingly alike (Waters 1991). Thus, there would seem to be an emerging consensus regarding the basic shape of the class system of modern societies. Following Giddens (1979), there are three main sources of class power: the possession of property, qualifications, and physical labour power, which tend to give rise to a three-class structure; a dominant/upper class based on property, an intermediate/middle class based on credentials, and a working/lower class based on labour-power. The neatness of this model is more apparent than real since the three classes may be internally divided into class fractions, the

cohesiveness of which may vary in time and space. This is arguably especially true for the middle class as it includes the propertied old middle class as well as the propertyless new middle class,
which in turn may be fragmented on the basis of cultural and
organization assets (Savage *et al*. 1992) and by employment sector
(Edgell and Duke 1991).

THE DOMINANT CLASS(ES)

Bias is built into the language of class. This is no more clearly
illustrated than in the case of the dominant classes. Neo-Marxists
talk about the capitalist classes, which implies exploitation, and/
or the ruling classes which implies that political power is cotermi-
nous with economic power. Neo-Weberians, on the other hand,
do not assume that economic power leads directly to political
power and consequently distinguish between those with economic
power (the positively privileged), and those with political power
(the governing class or political elite). Sociologists who operate
with a pure occupationally-based class model tend to refer to the
richest class as the upper class. The term dominant class is arguably one of the more neutral ways of designating those at the
apex of the class structure, although it does allude to the Marxist
theory of dominant ideology, which suggests that the 'ideas of
the ruling class are in every epoch the ruling ideas' (Marx and
Engels 1970: 64).

The origin of the debate about the fate of the dominant
classes this century can be traced back to Marx and Weber. Both
social theorists noted that capitalist development involved the
separation of ownership from control due to the increased size
and complexity of companies, but emphasized slightly different
aspects of the change. For example, for Marx the tendency for
the 'work of supervision' to become divorced from the 'ownership
of capital' meant that the capitalist was now 'superfluous' (1974:
386–8). Weber, on the other hand, claimed that the separation
of functions 'permits the selection for managerial posts of the
persons best qualified from the standpoint of profitability' (1964:
248–9). Since Marx and Weber in Europe, and others in America,
notably Veblen (1963), first noted the emergence of a managerial
class, the crucial question has become: what is the sociological
significance of this change in the class structure of modern
societies?

The variety of possible answers to this question have been

reviewed in detail by others, notably Nichols (1969) and Child (1969), hence here only the two basic positions will be considered. Managerialists have argued that the advent of managerial capitalism has transformed capitalism, including the class structure. Conversely, non-managerialists have taken the view that the separation of ownership from control has not altered the basic nature of capitalist society. Managerialists, who in the main are non-Marxists, and non-managerialists, who on the whole tend to be neo-Marxists, agree that control has been separated from ownership, but they differ markedly on the sociological interpretation of this historical change.

The major contributors to the managerialist view include Aron (1972), Berle and Means (1968), Burnham (1945), Crossland (1964), Dahrendorf (1959), and Galbraith (1967). In their various ways they assert that the managerial control of the modern corporation is different from capitalist control in two respects: it involves a shift in power from owners to managers, and managerial power is exercised in a more socially responsible way. For instance, in their pioneering empirical analysis of American capitalism Berle and Means documented what they regarded as the increasing separation of ownership from control in modern corporations. They claimed that there was a divergence of interest between ownership and control now that owners had been 'relegated to the position of those who supply the means whereby the new princes may exercise their power' (1968: 116). Finally, they hinted at the growth of a more socially responsible managerial class when they argued that:

> It is conceivable, – indeed it seems almost essential if the corporate system is to survive, – that the 'control' of the great corporations should develop into a purely neutral technocracy, balancing the claims by various groups in the community and assigning to each a portion of the income stream on the basis of public policy rather than private cupidity.
>
> (Berle and Means 1968: 312–13)

According to Dahrendorf, echoing many of the earlier managerialist writers, including Berle and Means, the main consequence of the separation of ownership from control is

> that it produces two sets of roles the incumbents of which increasingly move apart in their outlook on and attitudes

toward society in general, and toward the enterprise in particular. Their reference groups differ, and different reference groups make for different values . . . Never has the imputation of the profit motive been further from the real motives of men than it is for modern bureaucratic managers. Economically, managers are interested in such things as rentability, efficiency and productivity.

(1959: 46)

Dahrendorf advances his thesis that managers are quite different from owner-managers with reference to the importance of the bureaucratic career in relation to both social origins and occupational experience, but with a minimum of empirical evidence. In other words, in the context of the growth of corporations and the dispersion of ownership, he asserts that the separation of ownership from control leads to the emergence of a new class of managers who exercise authority on the basis of their professional credentials and/or their organizational position. He concludes that since labour is no longer confronted by a homogeneous capitalist class, he doubts that it 'can still be described as class conflict' (Dahrendorf 1959: 48). Thus, Dahrendorf, along with other managerialists, is a post-capitalist, industrial society theorist rather than a capitalist society theorist (Scott 1985).

Nichols has argued that although it is possible to distinguish a variety of managerialist traditions, they all share the view that not only has a separation of ownership and control occurred, but that: 'they believe that it matters, and that it has resulted in changes in business behaviour and, by extension, business ideology' (1969: 55).

Non-managerialists tend to be less heterogeneous than managerialists in the sense that they all follow Marx to a greater or lesser extent (Baran and Sweezy 1968; Blackburn 1965; De Vroey 1975; Miliband 1973; Westergaard and Resler 1975; Zeitlin 1989; McDermott 1991). Non-managerialists contend that even if ownership has been divorced from control, this change in the structure of capitalist enterprises from personal to impersonal forms of ownership does not alter the underlying nature of industrial capitalism, still less indicate the demise of the capitalist class. Several reasons and not a little evidence can be advanced in support of this thesis.

First, there is what Blackburn (1965: 117) has called the 'economic logic of the market' argument which reiterates Marx's basic point that: 'Competition makes the immanent laws of capitalist production to be felt by each individual capitalist, as external coercive laws' (1970a: 592). That is to say, in a free market system all corporations, irrespective of whether or not they are 'controlled' by owner-managers or professional managers, are constrained to make a profit or risk extinction.

Second, the thrust of this critique of managerialism is reinforced by two further points which focus on the social and economic unity of owners and managers. Research on corporations in Britain and many other industrial capitalist societies has been thoroughly reviewed by Scott (1985). This shows that managers and owners come from similar social backgrounds in terms of their class origins and educational experiences, and that there is a tendency for managers to own shares in their own company and hence derive a proportion of their income from this source. Drawing upon the work of Bourdieu (1971), Scott has argued that whereas the direct inheritance of corporate power was the norm in the past under the personal mode of domination, it is now supplemented by indirect social mechanisms involving the purchase of privileged education. This enables the capitalist class to pass on to their offspring cultural capital as well as economic capital. Thus, the growth of impersonal capitalism 'has resulted merely in a managerial reorganization of the capitalist class' (Scott 1985: 256).

Third, contemporary data shows that professional managers are recruited, retained and promoted for their ability to produce profits (Nichols 1969; Zeitlin 1989; McDermott 1991). Unsurprisingly, one study of professional managers concluded that: 'Not only were they more oriented to profit, they were more capable of obtaining it' (Pahl and Winkler 1974: 118). This research finding raises major doubts about the validity of the distinction between 'management' and 'owner' controlled firms that is at the core of the managerialist thesis.

These criticisms of managerialism suggest that the separation of ownership and control has not led to the 'disappearance of the capitalist class', but to its 'transformation' as private property has assumed an increasingly corporate form (Scott 1991: 24). Thus, notwithstanding the difficulty of identifying this small but significant class – hence Goldthorpe's 'rather anomalous' inclusion of large proprietors in his service class (Erikson and Goldthorpe 1992: 40) – the capitalist class has survived the change from individual to collective forms of ownership and control.

According to Scott, the modern capitalist business class may be divided into four analytically 'distinct class segments' (1991: 72): The entrepreneurial capitalist (i.e. the classical capitalist owner who actively controls all aspects of a business), the rentier capitalist (i.e. the absentee owner who passively collects dividends), the executive capitalist (i.e. the bureaucratic capitalist who may or may not be propertyless), and the finance capitalist (i.e. the occupier of multiple directorships, often on a part-time basis, who may or may not be propertyless). Thus, the modern capitalist class 'consists of those whose family wealth and life chances are generated by the involvement of their members in these capitalist economic locations' (Scott 1991: 72).

If the managerial revolution is a 'pseudofact' (Zeitlin 1989: 156), what evidence is there for the existence of a politically dominant capitalist class? Research in America (Domhoff 1967) and in Britain (Scott 1991), suggests that the concept of the ruling class is still relevant to a sociological understanding of the 'top' of the class structure.

Building on a strong sociological tradition, exemplified by the work of Mills (1968), Domhoff reviewed previous research methods and findings, added some material of his own and came to the conclusion that the American upper class is a governing class. He summarized the differences between the two basic modes of analysis of dominant classes as follows:

> The decision-making approach is concerned with issues and attempts to study the decision-making process and its outcome. The sociology-of-leadership methodology is concerned with sociological background and studies the sociological composition of institutional leadership and of decision-making groups. The decision-making method has trouble specifying key political issues, the real interests of the protagonists, the factors involved in the decision, and the long-run consequences of the outcome; the sociology-of-leadership method runs into trouble demonstrating that upper-class leaders have special interests and specifying how many decision-makers and institutional leaders must be members of the upper class.
>
> (Domhoff 1967: 145–6)

Domhoff noted that both methods are imperfect and in his own study emphasized the sociology-of-leadership approach on three main grounds:

1 that it is easier to agree about the major institutions of American society (e.g. elite educational, social, economic and political institutions) than about the interests of various classes;

2 that it is very difficult to study decision-making compared to ascertaining the social composition of a leadership group;

3 that the criticism of the sociology-of-leadership method regarding the specific interests of upper-class leaders can be answered in part by revealing that this class own a disproportionate proportion of a nation state's wealth, and 'receive a disproportionate amount of yearly income' (Domhoff 1967: 146).

Domhoff's key conclusion was 'that the income, wealth, and institutional leadership' of an empirically identifiable American upper class 'is sufficient to earn it the designation "governing class" ' (1967: 156).

With the exception a few small-scale sociological studies, such as those by Lupton and Wilson (1959) and Nichols (1969), it was not until the recent research by Scott (1982; 1985 and 1991) that the issue of the existence of a ruling class could be answered satisfactorily on the basis of empirical evidence. In his latest and most readable study, Scott has written a British sequel to Domhoff's justly famous book in which he agrees with the neo-Marxist view (cf. Miliband 1973) that 'there is in Britain today a ruling class' (1991: 3–4).

First, Scott addressed the question: what is a capitalist class? His answer was that it may be defined as an economically dominant class which derives its advantages from the ownership and control of private property, and which has 'distinct and opposing interests to those of the other classes' (1991: 7). As noted above, he claims that changes in the structure of business organizations have transformed this class from one based on the 'personal' ownership of capital to one based increasingly on the less easily identifiable 'impersonal' ownership. Despite this important change, it is still possible to identify a capitalist class in Britain 'whose members are dependent on the success of the system of capitalist private property which produces its income and wealth' (Scott 1991: 24). Class reproduction is in part a direct consequence of private ownership and control, and in part an indirect consequence of social networks rooted in family and education.

Scott's next step is to show that the dominant economic class is also dominant politically, i.e. exercises state power. He argues that:

> A capitalist class may be regarded as forming a ruling class when its economic dominance is sustained by the operations of the state and when, alone or through a wider power bloc, it is disproportionately represented in the power elite which rules the state apparatus.
>
> (Scott 1991: 38)

On the basis of social background data, or what Domhoff refers to as the sociology-of-leadership methodology, Scott 'affirms the existence of a power bloc: an alliance of classes rooted in the unifying features of distinct patterns of social background . . . within which a capitalist business class holds the dominant position' (1991: 137).

Having demonstrated that the capitalist class rules politically, Scott considered the 'mechanisms through which this political domination can be achieved' (1991: 139). He suggests that the state operates in favour of the capitalist class and that this is not a matter of exclusive advantage but relative advantage in the sense that its activities support, rather than undermine, the existing capitalist social relations and hence the interests of the capitalist class. Thus, for Scott, the basic economic, legal and normative structure of capitalist Britain 'have never been renegotiated through the decision-making apparatus of the state' (1991: 142). In other words, the state is historically and structurally biased in ways that favour the continued economic and political dominance of the capitalist class.

Scott concluded that Britain has a ruling class 'whose economic dominance is sustained by the operations of the state and whose members are disproportionately represented in the power elite which rules the state apparatus' and that under certain conditions the role of the state is more important in ensuring class domination than class background (1991: 151).

In contrast to managerialists who subscribe to an industrial society model of societal development, anti-managerialists claim that capitalism has not been transformed beyond recognition, although it has changed. Ownership has been depersonalized, not abolished. Strategic control (i.e. long-term planning) has been retained; only operational control (i.e. medium and short-term implementation of basic long-term goals) has been relinquished

(Scott 1985; Clegg *et al.* 1986). The profit motive, the motor of capitalist development, has not become less important. The economic power of the capitalist class has increased as a result of the growth of international corporations, and continuity is achieved by a combination of the monopolization of wealth and educational privileges. This has led Scott to conclude that: 'The managerial revolution, far from nearing completion, has not yet begun' (1985: 260).

At this stage in the analysis a question arises: how is it possible for a relatively small ruling class to monopolize wealth and power in democratic societies characterized by massive inequality and periodic economic crises? One possible answer to this question is to argue that the economic and political dominance of the capitalist class is legitimized by reference to ideas that serve its interests, and which are thought to be widely shared by other classes. This consensual dimension of capitalist class domination is the other sense in which Marx and Engels used the term ruling class, although they did not explain the distinction between the political and intellectual expressions of ruling class domination 'systematically' (Bottomore 1991: 485).

Following Gramsci (1971), the class domination of civil society is referred to as hegemony, and is known more generally in Marxist theory as the dominant ideology thesis, i.e. the existence of a powerful dominant class ideology that stresses the virtue of private property creates an acceptance of the whole capitalist social order among all classes. However, this has been shown to be an exceedingly complex and problematic proposition in that it is predicated on an 'over-socialised conception of society' and a corresponding emphasis on the ideological incorporation of the subordinate classes, and also because the improvement in the mechanisms of transmission, notably the growth of mass education and the mass media, has coincided in late capitalism with a decline in the coherence of the dominant ideology (Abercrombie *et al.* 1980: 152). More specifically, first, it has been noted that there is a tension between key elements of the dominant ideology such as ascriptive privileges, associated with the right to own and inherit private property and achieved privileges, associated with credentialism and bureaucratization (Abercrombie *et al.* 1980). Second, it has been argued by Abercrombie *et al.* (1980) that subordinate class integration has more to do with what Marx called the 'dull compulsion of economic relations' (1970a: 737), and 'pragmatic acceptance' (Mann 1973: 30) of the status quo, than with shared values. Third, and not unrelatedly, Veblen has highlighted the conservative political force of the 'struggle for pecuniary reputability' via emulatory conspicuous consumption (1970: 39; see also Edgell 1992). Fourth, Veblen has also emphasized the social solidarity that flows from patriotism (1964), plus the 'psychic income' that is generated by successful imperialism and shared by all classes (1964: 71; see also Edgell and Townshend 1992). Fifth, in the event of the reward system and reformism failing, direct force or political repression can be used against dissenting subordinates to regain control and maintain order (Miliband 1989). It is thought that physical coercion is more common during the transition to industrial capitalism and that economic dependence characterizes advanced societies (Abercrombie *et al.* 1980). Moreover, it has been shown that during the 1980s in Britain (and elsewhere) there was a recrudescence of essential capitalist values which increased the internal coherence of the dominant ideology and capitalist class support for it (Edgell and Duke 1991). This suggests that: 'The capitalist class is dominant economically, politically and culturally' (Bottomore 1989: 10).

THE INTERMEDIATE CLASS(ES)

During this century the class locations in the middle of the class structure of modern capitalist societies are thought to have expanded and fragmented more than any other, and as a consequence, are typically regarded as 'one of the most intractable issues in contemporary sociology' (Abercrombie and Urry 1983: 1). Conventionally, a historically and theoretically sensitive distinction is made between the 'old' propertied and the 'new' propertyless 'middle classes' (cf. Mills 1956); they are also known as the small or petit bourgeoisie and the white-collar or non-manual classes. The former can include the self-employed with and without employees, and the latter can range from white-collar workers with modest authority to highly credentialized professionals. This dualistic conception of the heterogeneous middle class will be the basis of presenting the material on this most problematic of classes.

The old middle class

The 'old' entrepreneurial middle class are distinctive in that they simultaneously own and work the means of production, and sometimes employ others, typically relatives. Marx and Weber referred to this class as the 'lower strata of the middle class' and the 'lower middle class' respectively and both expected this class to be extinguished by the fire of competition from big capitalists (Marx and Engels 1848: 62–3; Weber 1964: 427). However, whereas Marx emphasized their decline into the expanding proletariat, Weber argued that their best option in the future was to become technically trained. This is an early version of what was to become a major debate in the sociology of class, namely proletarianization versus embourgeoisement. What has happened is that although large companies now dominate the modern economy, especially the manufacturing sector, small businesses have not only survived but expanded, particularly in the service sector (Bogenhold and Staber 1991; Burrows and Curran 1989; Scase and Goffee 1980; Storey 1983; Wright 1985; Steinwetz and Wright 1989).

Notwithstanding the diversity inherent within the entrepreneurial middle class (cf. Goss 1991), e.g. the self-employed, small employers, owner-controllers and owner-directors, Scase and Goffee (1982) have identified three distinct approaches to this class. The first emphasizes terminal decline, so I have called it *demise theory*, the second concentrates on survival and may therefore be described as *marginalization theory*, and the third claims that small is increasingly beautiful, hence the label *de-marginalization theory*.

Until recently the historical evidence seemed to confirm neo-Marxist demise theory. Between 1960 and 1980 US census data showed that small-scale capitalism declined from 13.8 per cent to 9.3 per cent of the labour force (Wright and Martin 1987). Similarly, in the UK between 1970 and 1979 the official number of self-employed declined from 2 million to 1.9 million (Brown 1990). However, during the 1980s the small business sector increased in many western societies (Loutfi 1991). For example, in Britain self-employment increased by around 50 per cent over the decade (Brown 1990) and this reversal of the historical trend was not unconnected with Conservative government measures aimed at encouraging self-employment (e.g. the Enterprise Allowance Scheme) as part of a wider policy to combat rising unemployment (Curran *et al.* 1986). It also coincided with the growth of the flexible firm and the strategy of using subcontractors (Hakim 1988). It is too early to tell whether this a new long-term trend or a short-term pattern.

In terminology reminiscent of Mills, who described the declining old middle class as the 'lumpen-bourgeoisie' (1956: 28), Gerry has speculated on the class implications of the growth of petty capitalism by noting that the movement of redundant wage workers into self-employment characterized by insecurity, long hours, poor conditions and low profits represents the emergence of a 'disguised proletariat' (1985: 188). Thus, part of the working class may be disappearing into self-employment, but they are not escaping from exploitation and oppression since their changed class situation is comparable to their previous one. However, this change in employment status, which is now individualist rather than collectivist, is related in Britain and America to a tendency to support right-wing political parties (Bechhofer and Elliot 1978; Form 1982). Consequently, neo-Marxist demise theory cannot be rejected out of hand. The declining old middle class has been replaced in part by an expanding working class, albeit in a disguised form.

The persistence of the old middle class as a marginal class that stands 'outside' a class structure dominated by big capital and organized labour, and which is threatened by both, is a perspective that predates the recent revival of this class (Bechhofer *et al.* 1974; Bechhofer and Elliot 1981). The survival of this class is explained with reference to economic forces, such as the transmission of property, the attraction of escape from subordination and relative wealth, the creation of new opportunities that invariably accompany the business cycle and technological change; and political forces, notably the recognition by governments that petty capitalism performs crucial ideological as well as economic functions. In other words, encouraging new enterprises is an ideologically sound way of absorbing some of the growth in unemployment and cutting state expenditure. This argument is congruent with the working unemployed thesis advanced by Henry (1982), in which he drew attention to the informal sector of the economy that is thought to expand during a recession as redundant workers adopt 'off the books' survival strategies. Taken together, the durability of small-scale capitalism, on a formal or informal basis, is a theory that consigns this class to permanent marginality.

The third perspective is the most optimistic, in that it regards the old middle class as an expanding prototypical class rather than as a declining or static atypical class. Moreover, it is the most recent theory to emerge and therefore has topical plausibility. The assertion that the entrepreneurial middle class will become more common in the future is based on a positive interpretation of certain social trends. First, the transition from a manufacturing to a service economy favours the growth of petit capitalism due to its labour- rather than capital-intensive nature (Institute of Employment Research 1987)). Second, small business growth is facilitated by technological changes that render once relatively expensive capital, notably computers, available to all (Scase and Goffee 1982). Third, there is the quality of life argument that small is more worker and environmentally friendly than big business (Boissevain 1984). Fourth, in the historical context of a revived enterprise culture, the small business becomes a fashionable ideal and is perceived as a mobility opportunity that is favoured by right-wing government policy (Burrows 1991; Goss 1991). Finally, there is the growth of cooperatives (i.e collective self-employment) as a response to unemployment or an alternative to work within a bureaucratic hierarchy (Cornforth *et al.* 1988). This theory implies that the current revival of all kinds of small capitalism will continue in the future and that the old middle class will thus become a more important class. This view tends to discount the fact that small-scale capitalism is notoriously risky (Hudson 1989), hence the continued growth of the 'old' middle class is far from assured.

It is difficult to generalize about a class that may be 'united' by employment status, but which contains a diversity of class situations (Curran and Burrows 1986). Each of the theories reviewed focuses on different aspects of the old middle class; demise theory emphasizes the working conditions of the weaker elements of this class, marginalization theory focuses on the factors that account for its persistence, and demarginalization theory concentrates on the factors that favour growth. A recent comparative analysis concluded that: 'Rising rates of self-employment are more likely a reflection of labour market deficiencies than a development contributing to their solution' (Bogenhold and Staber 1991: 235). This suggests that marginalization theory, which rules out terminal decline and unlimited growth, is the most promising theory regarding the future of this intermediate class. Certainly, the historical decline of the old middle class seems to have come to an end, 'at least temporarily' (Steinmetz and Wright 1989).

The new middle class

The new middle class refers to white-collar employees and once again current debates on changes within this class can be traced back to Marx and Weber's seminal contributions to class analysis. According to Marx, white-collar workers 'belong to a better paid class of wage-workers', and due to the advance of the 'division of labour in the office' and the 'universality of public education', the supply of this type of worker would increase and their wage would fall (1974: 300). In contrast to Marx's 'devaluation' or proletarianization thesis, Weber expected the opposite trend to prevail. He argued that the 'increasing bureaucratization of administration enhances the importance of the specialist examination', and that the consequent 'universal clamor for the creation of educational certificates in all fields makes for the formation of a privileged stratum in bureaus and in offices' (1961: 241). Thus Marx and Weber both noted the emerging growth of white-collar workers, but interpreted this trend differently.

In numerical terms, Marx and Weber were both correct to anticipate the expansion of white-collar groups. For example in Britain between 1911 and 1981 white-collar workers (i.e. professional, managerial, supervisory and clerical) increased from under 14 per cent of the occupied population to over 43 per cent (Routh 1987). A similar change has occurred in the USA; between 1900 and 1980 white-collar workers (i.e. proprietors, professional, managerial, sales and clerical) increased from 17.5 per cent to over 52 per cent of the labour force (Gilbert and Kahl 1987).

The key question is how to interpret this change in the 'middle' of the class structure. One possibility is to argue that Marx's thesis has been confirmed by the declining class situation of clerical workers, and Weber's thesis by the improving class situation of professional workers (Abercrombie and Urry 1983). In other words, Marx and Weber were both correct; the new middle class has split into two distinct groups, a deskilled routine white-collar fraction and an enskilled specialist fraction.

Braverman has addressed two of Marx's three forms of proletarianization, that of society and work (see Chapter 1), with special reference to routine white-collar occupations. He claimed that the massive expansion during this century of clerical work in Britain and the United States is part of the proletarianization of both manual and mental labour in society. He argued that in contrast to today, the 'function, authority, pay, tenure and employment prospects' of clerks used to be 'closer to the employer than to factory labor' (Braverman 1974: 295). In other words, the class situation of clerical workers has declined following the bureaucratization, rationalization and feminization of office work. In developing his neo-Marxist thesis, Braverman challenged the view that the routine non-manual worker was a member of the middle class in monopoly capitalism:

> If one ascribes to the millions of present-day clerical workers the "middle class" or semi-managerial functions of that tiny and long-vanished clerical stratum of early capitalism, the result can only be a drastic misconception of modern society.
>
> (1974: 293)

Braverman's thesis stimulated a great deal of research and became the focus of critical debate in both the sociology of work and class (cf. Littler and Salaman 1984; Thompson 1983; Wood 1983). The most relevant criticisms in terms of the present discussion are that, first, Braverman's craft perspective, which informs his theory of deskilling of both manual and non-manual work, involves a mistaken conception of nineteenth-century craft work (Cutler 1978). For example, historical research on clerks has shown that his portrayal of Victorian clerks as semi-managerial craft workers is false because it emphasizes in a selective way the more skilled aspects of clerical work at the expense of the less skilled tasks (Attewell 1989).

Second, Braverman's claim that both manual and non-manual work have been deskilled during the twentieth century fails to recognize that deskilling is an uneven process (Penn and Scattergood 1985; Lowe 1987). Research also shows that in addition to the process of clerical deskilling highlighted by Braverman, technological changes such as computerization can also involve enskilling (Crompton and Reid 1983; Gallie 1991).

Third, and relatedly, it has been noted that the debate about proletarianization 'has suffered from a heavy reliance on case studies of unknown typicality' (Gallie 1991: 337). When more

representative national census and other data have been considered they fails to confirm the degrading of work dimension
of the proletarianization thesis (Goldthorpe 1987; Gallie 1991).
However, although upskilling is far more prevalent than deskilling, Gallie's evidence suggests that 'men have benefited to a
considerably greater extent than women from the process of
upskilling' (1991: 343).

Fourth, and finally, Braverman has been criticized for his
overly 'deterministic' and 'one-sided' account of class in which
an all-powerful capitalist class dominates a totally malleable
working class (e.g. MacKenzie 1977). Consequently, his theory
of increasing class homogenization is unable to explain variations
in either class consciousness or class action, including unionization in general and white-collar unionization in particular (Price
and Bain 1983; Hyman and Price 1983). In other words, Braverman has been criticized for neglecting to consider Marx's crucial
third form of proletarianization, the political radicalization of
workers associated with the degradation of work.

However, Braverman is not alone in advancing the thesis
that routine white-collar workers have been proletarianized in
certain respects. The American sociologists, Mills (1956) and
Aronowitz (1974) have both claimed that historically, white-collar
work has been deskilled due to the impact of mechanization and
bureaucratization, and that consequently working in an office is
little different from working in a factory. More recently, Wright
and Singelmann (1982) initially and tentatively argued on the
basis of US national data that the proletarianization tendency
was more marked than the de-proletarianization tendency. However, in later articles they came to the opposite conclusion (Singelmann and Tienda 1985; Wright and Martin 1987), but seemed
reluctant to abandon the proletarianization thesis altogether.
They suggested that it was a matter of international rather than
national trends in the sense that there was the possibility that a
process of upgrading was occurring in the 'core capitalist countries' and of downgrading in the Third World (Wright and Martin
1987: 23).

In Britain, Westergaard and Resler have argued on the basis
of relative pay and control at work that (male) 'low-grade office
and sales employees' have experienced proletarianization during
this century (1975: 75). Moreover, in terms of 'official class'
position or social standing, between 1911 and 1931 clerks were
relegated from class I to class III (Hakim 1980). This was a

period during which there was a threefold increase in the number of clerical workers, the vast majority of whom were women, office work became mechanized, and typing pools were introduced (McNally 1979). Thus, the proletarianization of office work coincided with the feminization of office workers. The spatial division of labour argument that deskilled workers are increasingly located in the Third World has also been advanced with reference to the restructuring of Britain (Abercrombie and Urry 1983).

An alternative to the neo-Marxist thesis of white-collar proletarianization can be found in the work of Lockwood (1958). On the basis of his distinction between work, market and status situations Lockwood showed that despite the bureaucratization and rationalization of office work, compared with manual workers, male clerks still enjoy closer social and physical proximity to authority, better pay and promotion prospects, and more status. He concluded that although the clerk shares with manual workers a 'propertyless status', the proletarianization of work and society theses must be rejected since in many other respects, the clerk has retained a superior position in the class and status structure. In contrast to Braverman, Lockwood also addressed the political proletarianization thesis. He found that variations in the class situation of clerical workers were associated with a great 'diversity' of class consciousness (Lockwood 1958: 211). Consequently, Lockwood also concluded that the Marxist theory of false consciousness did not apply to clerical workers.

In a long postscript to a new edition of his original book, Lockwood reviewed the class situation of clerks in the light of subsequent research and once again rejected all three forms of the neo-Marxist theory of proletarianization with respect to the routine non-manual worker (1989). Conversely, he re-emphasized, the link between variations in class situation and class consciousness, and on the basis of 'rather patchy' data, he suggested two possibilities:

> The firmer one is that, regardless of the extent to which clerical work may be said to have been proletarianized, there are no grounds for thinking that the majority of clerical workers have experienced proletarianization. The promotion opportunities of male clerks and the fairly rapid turnover of female clerks more or less guarantee that this is not the case. Secondly, the view that clerical

work itself has undergone widespread "degradation", as a result of rationalization and mechanization, is not one that has found much support. Indeed, the most detailed recent surveys and case-studies of the effects of the new technology lead to just the opposite conclusion: namely, that reskilling, even job enrichment appear to be the most general consequences.

(Lockwood 1989: 250)

Support for Lockwood's position has come from Goldthorpe, who has stated that 'in Britain at least, the thesis of white-collar proletarianisation is likely to prove as empirically questionable as that of working class embourgeoisement' (1972: 355; see also Goldthorpe and Bevan 1977: 312). More recently Goldthorpe and Erikson have argued that mobility data is crucial to proletarianization theory in two related respects: 'It has to be shown both that degraded jobs are held by individuals "forced down" from more advanced positions and that these individuals then have little chance of escaping such jobs' (1992: 13). As far as routine non-manual workers are concerned, research by Stewart *et al.* (1980) and Marshall *et al.* (1988), among others, shows that this is not the case.

In order to clarify the debate regarding white-collar proletarianization the gender dimension would seem to be central. This is because it has been argued that men have tended to benefit from the growth of enskilled jobs at the expense of women, who are over-represented in deskilled clerical work (Crompton and Jones 1984). Even the Stewart *et al.* study of male clerks contrasted the location of women in the 'most menial clerical tasks with limited opportunities for promotion' and the 'routine' nature of male clerical promotion (1980: 94). Similarly, Marshall *et al.*, who reject all other versions of the proletarianization thesis, noted that 'women engaged in rank-and-file service employment may perform routinized tasks that render their work more or less indistinguishable from those typical of manual employees' (1988: 136). However, to claim that this gender version of the proletarianization thesis is valid, it would need to be shown that women have experienced the proletarianization of office work. In fact, very few women have 'because their recruitment was directly linked to the proliferation' of routine administrative tasks (Lowe 1987: 143–4).

However, some jobs and some people, (especially 'women's

work'), have been proletarianized and this has led Giddens to conclude that 'women are in a sense the "underclass" of the white-collar sector' (1979: 288). Thus, the safest conclusion is that as far as the proletarianization of the lower middle class is concerned, the major tendency is male enskilling and the minor tendency is female deskilling (Abercrombie and Urry 1983). This suggests that although the evidence supports the thesis of a general upgrading throughout the occupational class structure of advanced societies, a process of polarization would seem to be occurring within and between societies and is related to technological change (cf. Gallie 1991). Thus, just when the proletarianization debate appears to be resolved in favour of the non-Marxists (Crompton 1990), the growth of the secondary labour market, notably casualization, and all this implies for polarization in housing (Ford 1989), as well as in work (Gallie 1991), suggests that proletarianization is a complex and not entirely a dead issue.

The other part of the new middle class comprises managerial and professional workers who have not only grown in number, but are also thought to have improved their class situation over the past century. Although the historical transformation of this fraction of the new middle class in quantitative and qualitative terms is not in question (cf. Abercrombie and Urry 1983; Gilbert and Kahl 1987; Routh 1987; Wright and Martin 1987), there are competing explanations of how this came about. Neo-Marxists such as Carter (1985) tend to refer to the concentration of capital, the increased importance of management, and hence the role of managers in the class structure. Neo-Weberians on the other hand, like Parkin (1979), point to the professionalization of work, the increased importance of formal qualifications, and hence the role of professionals in the class structure. The term that is used to indicate the rise of both the managerial and professional elements of the new middle class is the service class (see Chapter 2). In view of the mixed intellectual pedigree of this concept, it is entirely appropriate that Abercrombie and Urry (1983) should draw upon this concept to provide an integrated neo-Marxist and neo-Weberian account of the new middle classes.

For Abercrombie and Urry, the service class can be analysed in neo-Weberian terms in that it refers to the 'upper' part of the new middle class that may be distinguished from deskilled white-collar places by virtue of a relatively privileged work and market situation (1983: 118–22), and in neo-Marxist terms because it 'performs the functions of control, reproduction and conceptualization – necessary functions for capital in relation to labour' (1983: 122). Typically, this class is recruited by bureaucracies on the basis of credentials. Those in service class places have careers and enjoy all the associated benefits such as authority and auton- omy, plus regular improvements in pay and conditions as they progress up the bureaucratic hierarchy. As far as relations between the service class and other classes are concerned, Aber- crombie and Urry suggest that capital has been 'weakened' by the managerial reorganization and concomitant depersonalization of capital and labour 'because of the processes by which knowl- edge, skill and control have been separated off and embodied within distinct middle-class places' (1983: 132). They concluded that 'although it is incorrect to see the service class as a potential ruling class', the power of this class has been developed 'at the expense of both capital and, especially, labour' (1983: 151). The argument stops just short of claiming that the service class has displaced the capitalist class, rather, it is asserted that the func- tions of both these classes 'are becoming somewhat indistinguish- able' (1983: 153: see also Lash and Urry 1987).

The claim by Abercrombie and Urry that: 'It makes less and less sense, therefore, to refer to the service class as a class "in the middle" ' (1983: 124), is similar to Goldthorpe's (1987) use of the term to include higher-grade employees and large owners (see Chapter 2). Yet Goldthorpe has also described the service class as 'a class who are subordinate to some form of higher agency' (1982: 180). Notwithstanding the last point, these sociol- ogists seem to be suggesting that the service class is not an intermediate class but a dominant one. In order to sustain this position it is not enough to point to the 'weakening' of capital, a questionable thesis in its own right (see pp. 56–8), it is necessary to show that the bases of service class power – organizational and educational assets – are comparable to the power of property, and that at the apex of corporations there is an overlap among those who occupy the various capitalist locations. Whilst the latter may well be the case (cf. Scott 1991), organizational and cultural assets are inferior to property as sources of class power (Savage et al. 1992). Specifically, it is argued by Savage et al. that property is the strongest basis of class formation since it can be accumu- lated, stored and transmitted with ease, whereas cultural assets can be stored but can only be realized in an organizational setting and are the subject of what Collins has called an 'inflationary struggle' (1979: 193). Organizational assets do not have the security of either property or credentials, yet retain the potential to generate considerable rewards.

The distinction between property, organizational and cultural assets developed by Savage *et al.* (1992) reveals the diversity of class situations characteristic of the so-called 'service class' and raises doubts about its alleged class unity and conservatism. Goldthorpe (1982) has suggested that members of the service class are unified by their similar class situation and trusted service relationship with their employers. Hence, they have a 'substantial stake in the status quo' and therefore constitute a 'conservative element within modern societies' (Goldthorpe 1982: 180). He contrasts his neo-Weberian view to neo-Marxist and 'new class' writers, such as Mallet (1975) and Gouldner (1979), who have argued that the service class could be radicalized by a recession. Although Goldthorpe is sceptical about this possibility, recent research shows that private sector controllers tend to be more conservative than public sector controllers and that the latter were radicalized by cuts in public spending in Britain during the 1980s (Edgell and Duke 1986 and 1991).

It would seem that Abercrombie and Urry's (1983) analysis of the new middle class is more helpful in clarifying the boundary between female-dominated routine and male-dominated specialized white-collar work than it is in differentiating between the service class and the capitalist class. In contrast to the view that the professional/managerial new middle class are part of a dominant service class, Savage *et al.* (1992) emphasize the advantages of cultural assets over organizational assets, and the advantage of property assets over both. Thus, the fragmentation of the middle class is captured systematically and clearly by the identification of three class assets – property, cultural and organizational – which provide the basis of three middle classes – the entrepreneurial, the professional and the managerial. However, the significance of these different types of assets varies historically and spatially, and therefore influences the process of middle-class formation in any one society at any point of time (Savage *et al.* 1992).

THE SUBORDINATE CLASS(ES)

Conventionally, the subordinate classes are referred to as the working class, and invariably this is operationalized as manual employees. Whatever label is used and however it is defined, this class has been the major focus of class research and most of this effort has been concerned with the question: what has happened to the working class since Marx argued that their historical role was to overthrow the capitalist mode of production and establish a classless form of society?

According to Marx, revolutionary progress would occur where industrial capitalism is most advanced: 'The country that is more developed industrially only shows, to the less developed, the image of its own future' (1970a: 8–9). During this century America has been the major capitalist economy and should therefore contain the most revolutionary working class. Yet America is usually portrayed as the most advanced industrial society with the least developed proletariat (Lipset 1969). This apparent paradox has been the subject of much research and debate since the German sociologist Sombart first asked the question in 1906 in the form of a book title: 'Why is there no socialism in the United States?' (1976).

Sombart's point of departure was the Marxian thesis that capitalism would lead to socialism and he considered that the United States provided 'the classic case' for examining this key point of the Marxian theory of social change (1976: 15). Sombart searched for evidence of socialism and found little support for the Socialist Party of America. He also found that the American working class, individually and organizationally, was dominated by 'the spirit of business' in that they held an 'instrumental orientation' and lacked an 'oppositional consciousness' (1976: 17 and 21–22). Sombart concluded that in contrast to Europe, 'there is no Socialism in America' (1976: 23). This conclusion led Sombart to raise the issue of American exceptionalism first noted by Tocqueville over half a century earlier (1948), and the further question: 'Is America or Europe the "land of the future"?' (1976: 24).

Sombart's explanation of the conservatism of the American working class may be called a 'roast beef and apple pie' theory because he emphasized the relative prosperity of American workers in contrast to the relative poverty of European, especially German, workers (1976: 62–106). However, he also mentioned the extensive local and national democratization (1976: 29–32), the dominance of the established political parties (1976: 33–44), non-class social and political divisions such as ethnicity, race and region (1976: 49–51), patriotism (1976: 19 and 106), the absence of feudal institutions (1976: 109), minimal social distance between the classes (1976: 110), and last but not least, the role of an open frontier in creating both the possibility and ideology of upward social mobility (1976: 115–8). Sombart summed up his theory by noting that the American worker is 'much more favoured than his European counterpart' as a 'result of his political position and his economic situation – of a radical-democratic system of government and of a comfortable standard of living' (1976: 109). Somewhat surprisingly in view of the main thrust of his short book, at the end his study Sombart asserted that:

> All the factors that till now have prevented the develop-ment of Socialism in the United States are about to disappear or to be converted into their opposite, with the result that in the next generation Socialism in America will very probably experience the greatest possi-ble expansion of its appeal.
>
> (1976: 119)

Thus, Sombart accepted Marx's economic and political logic and argued that America was an exceptional case which would con-form in due course to the 'socialism follows capitalism' thesis.

The current debate regarding American exceptionalism, no doubt stimulated by the publication of the first full translation into English of Sombart's seminal study and by the contextual summary provided by Husbands (one of the two translators), shows no sign of waning (cf. Bottomore 1991; Piven and Cloward 1982; Ross 1991; Shafer 1991). Moreover, the argument that America is not the only advanced industrial capitalist society that has failed to fulfil Marx's expectation of an increasingly radical working class (Katznelson 1981) has led to a more detailed recon-sideration of the alleged distinctiveness of the class structure of American society.

Vanneman and Cannon (1987) have challenged one of the cornerstones of the conventional wisdom that what is exceptional about America is the limited class consciousness of the working class. They have argued, first, that the American labour move-ment may be comparatively small (currently less than one in five employed Americans are members of a trade union in contrast to about two in five in Britain), but that this does not mean that America is a class-conflict free zone. They assert that strikes in America tend to be longer and more violent than in other indus-trial capitalist societies. Second, they argue that in America the two main political parties both represent the interests of capital and that the lack of a leftist party is not unrelated to an exceptionally high level of working class non-voting (see Chapter 6). Third, on the basis of a definition of the working class that includes lower white-collar workers, their comparative analysis of class perceptions among white American and British employed male and employed female (or whose 'household heads' were economically active), workers, demonstrated that there is little difference in the class consciousness of the working class in the two countries. Fourth and finally, they argued that, 'what is exceptional about U.S. politics and about U.S. class conflict in general is the extraordinary power of U.S. capital' (Vanneman and Cannon 1987: 167). For example, in drawn-out labour-capital conflicts, 'capital rarely loses, partly because it has the financial resources to withstand enormous, if temporary losses' (Vanneman and Cannon 1987: 295). They concluded that it was a mistake to attribute the limited effectiveness of the American working class to a lack of class consciousness. Instead of 'blaming the victim', they suggested that 'even the most class conscious proletariat will not easily overcome a vigorous and united dominant class' (1987: 14). Thus, Vannemen and Cannon emphasized that it is not the class consciousness of the American proletariat that is distinctive, but the 'power of American capital' (1987: 291).

Although Vanneman and Cannon confirmed Sombart's view regarding the distinctiveness of America, they rejected his key economic explanation: 'The American Dream, in so far as it includes visions of comfort and affluence, is largely irrelevant to the course of class conflicts' (1987: 278). Moreover, their conclusions not only contradict the view advanced by Sombart, and by many other sociologists since, that the American working class is unusually conservative, but the main thrust of their analysis suggests that the conventional focus of class research should be reversed. In other words, rather than blame workers' subordination on their alleged lack of class consciousness, what is required 'is an appreciation of the power of capital as a variable feature of American society' (Vanneman and Cannon 1987: 292).

This challenging theory is somewhat speculative at the present time since little research has been undertaken that addresses directly the question of comparative (i.e. historical and cross-national) variations in the strength of the capitalist class. However, a recent empirical study of class consciousness and action in Britain during the Thatcher decade broadly supports Vanneman and Cannon's basic approach (Edgell and Duke 1991). This panel study found that under Thatcherism the balance of power between capital and labour altered in favour of capital. Notwithstanding this historical change in the relationship between the dominant and subordinate classes, there was plenty of evidence of the persistence of radical values, especially among workers and public sector managers. It concluded that 'the relatively acquiescent character of the propertyless classes during the 1980s was not unrelated to mass unemployment, changes in trade union law and the decline of public sector employment' (Edgell and Duke 1991: 213).

In the process of advancing their theory that American workers are as class conscious and class active as the working classes of other advanced societies, Vanneman and Cannon also commented on two other issues concerning class and social change, namely, embourgeoisement and ideological incorporation.

Regarding the widely discredited embourgeoisement thesis, they concurred with the critiques developed by Goldthorpe *et al.* (1968 and 1969) in Britain and Hamilton (1972) in America. (For an evaluation of the Affluent Worker project see Blackburn and Mann 1979; Devine 1992; Grieco 1981; Kemeny 1972; MacKenzie 1974; Westergaard 1970.) Vanneman and Cannon argued that the idea that affluence makes a difference 'confuses status and power'; a change in status or life-style does not alter a worker's subordinate class situation (1987: 275).

With respect to the role of ideology, in the light of their data on class consciousness and action, Vannemen and Cannon expressed scepticism about the dominant ideology thesis in relation to the working class. They suggested that, 'insofar as ideological hegemony refers to the internal cohesiveness of the dominant class and its hold over such closely allied groups as the middle class, it may explain some of the resilience of American capitalism' (Vanneman and Cannon 1987: 307). Following a review of the situation in Britain, as noted above, Abercrombie *et al.* (1980) came to a similar conclusion. They argued that the ideological incorporation of the working class in late capitalism has been overstated and that economic 'compulsion remains an important condition of system integration and of pragmatic apathy as an element of subordinate culture' (1980: 154). Edgell and Duke also support the Vanneman and Cannon line, in the sense that they found that the political and economic changes wrought by Thatcherism, 'reinforced the dominant values adhered to by the capitalist class' (1991: 212).

Finally, Vanneman and Cannon's American research is unusual in that it is informed by the distinction between social class and occupational prestige, whereas the American tradition of stratificational research has been dominated by the 'widespread and uncritical use of the term "socioeconomic status" rather than the term "class" ' (Waters 1991: 142). Most importantly, Vanneman and Cannon found that occupational status had less impact on 'class perception' than their three class variables (authority, mental labour and self-employment), particularly in the case of men (1991: 91). Thus, in Vanneman and Cannon's study, the dominant class, far from being obscured or ignored, is the focus of attention. Hence, in contrast to many others, they cannot be accused of testing a Marxian theory using a non-Marxist conception of class (Edgell and Duke 1986).

Marshall *et al.* are critical of all studies of individual class consciousness, such as those undertaken by Wright (1985), Vannemann and Cannon (1987), and Edgell and Duke (1991), since they claim that it is an 'attribute of organizations rather than individuals' (1988: 193). This reconceptualization of class consciousness is problematic, to say the least, because it tends to equate consciousness with action, whereas the class consciousness of individuals and the actions of organizations are distinct, albeit related phenomena (Evans 1992). It has also been suggested that the class consciousness needs to be disaggregated and not researched as if it were a unitary concept (Edgell and Duke 1991; Evans 1992).

The received wisdom that Britain is a class-divided society (cf. Marshall *et al.* 1988), and that America is exceptional in that it is not, can only be assessed meaningfully on the basis of cross-national data (Lipset 1991). In the absence of such data, Lipset's assertion that as other countries develop and 'Americanize', the United States will become less exceptional but never unexceptional, and will tend to prevail.

A NOTE ON THE UNDERCLASS

The ideologically loaded term the 'underclass' is often used to describe those at the bottom of the class structure who are persistently poor due to permanent or irregular economic inactivity, which in turn is often attributed to a culture of poverty and/or a cycle of deprivation rather than economic change (Bagguley and Mann 1992; Macnicol 1987; Morris 1989; Pahl 1984). Studies of class which focus on the economically active, by definition exclude the underclass from class analysis and imply that this 'class' is outside of 'society' (see Chapter 3). Yet for both Marx and Weber, the underclass was an integral part of the class system.

Marx referred to the underclass as a 'relative surplus population' or 'industrial reserve army' and argued that capital accumulation at one end of the class structure depended on the growth of a disposable labour force at the other (1970a: 632–3 and 644–5). In other words, wealth and poverty are two sides of the same coin; the underclass is a permanent feature of capitalism and not a temporary symptom of the business cycle. For Weber the underclass was a negatively privileged class which included 'outcasts', 'debtor classes' and the 'poor', some of whom may experience segregation on the basis of ethnic status (1964: 425; 1961).

Where (Marxian) labour market factors coincide with (Weberian) cultural features, the term underclass tends to become equated with inner-city Black populations. This has happened to a marked degree in America (Auletta 1982) and to an extent in Britain (Rex and Tomlinson 1979). However, this view implies that there is little variation in class terms within ethnic groups (Brown 1984), ignores the growth of female-headed single-parent families and elderly poor (Field 1989), and 'is prone towards the "ecological fallacy" ', i.e. the tendency to erroneously treat ecological correlations as guides to individual correlations (Bagguley and Mann 1992: 115).

An alternative thesis claims that: 'Since the underclass lacks any meaningful market position, it is best conceptualized as a social category, not a class' (Heisler 1991: 476). This approach to the underclass tends to confuse social marginality (i.e. citizenship element), with minimal and uneven labour market power (i.e. class element). It also tends to overlook the interconnectedness of wealth and poverty (i.e. the disposable labour-force role of the underclass), and the historical tendency for members of this class to riot (i.e. collective bargaining by force). Moreover, the growth of the underclass in America and Britain, due to economic recession, cuts in expenditure on social welfare, and deindustrialization, suggests that it is a regular feature of the class structure of advanced capitalist societies. Thus, it is arguably more constructive to regard the underclass as the underemployed and unemployed fraction of the working class, characterized, like all other classes, by a shifting population of variable size, but distinctive in its poverty.

SUMMARY AND CONCLUSIONS

Using a combination of neo-Marxist and neo-Weberian class theory, this chapter has considered three main class groupings – a dominant class of large property owners, a heterogeneous and expanding intermediate class based on petty property, organizational, and/or cultural assets, and a divided and possibly shrinking subordinate class that is dependent upon its ability to sell its physical labour power, plus the state to a greater or lesser extent. Although the basic structure of the class system of industrial capitalist societies, such as America and Britain, has remained the same during the twentieth century, there have been some important changes within and between the classes that make up the basic structure.

The smallest but most powerful class, the capitalist class, has experienced a decline in personal capital and a growth of impersonal forms of ownership. This has made it more difficult to identify this class, but this does not mean that it no longer exists or is any less powerful. The intermediate class has expanded and fragmented: the old propertied middle class has declined yet shows no sign of becoming extinct, whereas the new propertyless professional and managerial fractions have expanded in numbers and importance but have not usurped the power of the dominant class. Routine white-collar work has also expanded and is undertaken increasingly by women, and by men at the beginning of their careers. The class location of these workers is less and less a matter of dispute, as both neo-Marxist and neo-Weberian accounts consider that men in blue-collar jobs and women in routine white-collar jobs increasingly resemble each other in terms of their work and market situations. The extent of the convergence on this point can be judged from the following quotations:

> it seems almost certain that the large majority of white-collar employees, especially clerical and secretarial employees, have – at most – trivial autonomy on the job

and should therefore be placed within the working class itself.

(Wright 1978: 81)

women in routine clerical jobs are very closely comparable to men in manual wage-earning ones in that they occupy essentially subordinate positions within the organization of production, with negligible or at best strictly delimited autonomy and responsibility.

(Goldthorpe 1984: 495)

Among other things, this point underlines the declining significance of the distinction between manual and non-manual work. It also suggests that as far as modern capitalist societies are concerned, a limited version of the otherwise discredited proletarianization thesis may still be viable with special reference to women workers. However, this would seem to be a minor trend, whereas work has been upgraded throughout the occupational structure. This polarization may well become more pronounced as the secondary labour market expands and the conditions of employment (including security, prospects and pay) associated with it deteriorate. In the case of the subordinate class, it was argued that the failure of this class to fulfil Marx's expectation and effect revolutionary change reflected the strength of the capitalist class, especially in America, rather than a lack of working class consciousness. The interrelated theses of working-class ideological incorporation and embourgeoisement were rejected as theoretically and empirically unsound. Finally, an underclass, characterized by limited market capacity and therefore poverty, was found to be expanding, residing mainly in the inner city; and associated with ethnic disadvantage and intermittent violent protest.

At a descriptive level, once the Marxist theory of history is discarded, there would seem to be an emergent consensus among neo-Marxist and neo-Weberian class analysts. In order of economic importance, there are three distinct sources of class power, and hence three main classes: a dominant class based on the ownership of capital, an intermediate class based on the acquisition of educational and/or organizational assets, and a subordinate class based on the possession of physical labour. However, the coherence of this three-class model depends in large part upon the extent to which the classes identified are stable social formations, and therefore upon the patterning of mobility, and the degree to which the classes are related to the structuring of economic rewards and political preferences. These issues will be considered in the next two chapters.

5

Class and social mobility

INTRODUCTION

Social mobility refers to the movement of people between different classes. The hierarchical nature of class structures, even neo-Marxist ones, means that it is possible to define class improvement as upward mobility and class deterioration as downward mobility.

Marx (and Engels) were concerned with the political implications of both upward and downward social mobility. With reference to the latter, they wrote that the 'lower strata of the middle class . . . sink gradually into the proletariat', and then the proletariat 'raise[s] itself up' and overthrows the bourgeoisie (1848: 62 and 69–70). Regarding the politics of upward mobility, Marx noted that with the expansion of credit 'a man without fortune but possessing energy, solidity, ability and business acumen may become a capitalist . . . The more a ruling class is able to assimilate the foremost minds of a ruled class, the more stable and dangerous becomes its rule' (1974: 600–1). Interestingly, Marx and Engels also commented on the amount of social mobility in America. In 1852 Marx wrote that 'though classes already exist, they have not yet become fixed, but constantly change and inter-change their elements in constant flux' (1972: 18–9). Similarly, in the preface to the American edition of *The Condition of the Working-class in England*, Engels draw attention to the 'safety-valve' role of upward social mobility due to the 'easy access to the ownership of cheap land, and the influx of immigration' (1962: 6).

Weber's interest in social mobility was evident in his early research into the opportunities for upward social mobility among farm workers in eastern Germany. He concluded that the desire for independence was more important than purely 'economic considerations' (Bendix 1960: 46). This emphasis on the role of non-economic forces and the differential social mobility of Catholics and Protestants in Germany was the starting point of his famous thesis on the relationship between the Protestant ethic and the spirit of capitalism. Once again, Weber noted that the 'principal explanation of this difference must be sought in the permanent intrinsic character of their religious beliefs, and not only in their temporary external historico-political situations' (Weber 1976: 40).

Weber's interest in social mobility can also be discerned from his references to:

1 The number of classes 'between which an interchange of individuals on a personal basis or in the course of generations is readily possible and typically observable' (1964: 424).
2 The trend that: 'From one generation to another the most readily available path to advancement for skilled and semi-skilled workers is into the class of technically trained individuals' (1964: 427).
3 The suggestion that 'it is always important in studying occupational structure to know the system of social stratification, including the distribution of opportunity in the different classes and the types of education which are available for the various types of occupation requiring specialized training' (1964: 251).

Although Marx and Weber did not discuss social mobility directly or extensively, it pervades their respective analyses of class. In the case of Marx, Goldthorpe (1987) has noted the significance of mobility for his theory of class formation and action. Similarly, it can be argued that mobility was an important theme in Weber's analysis of social stratification, the occupational structure, and cultural values.

The influence of both Marx and Weber is evident in the first modern study of social mobility by the Russian-born American, Sorokin (1964). It was first published in 1927 and adopted an essentially neo-Weberian approach to social mobility in order to address Marx's theory of class. More specifically, Sorokin distinguished between economic, occupational and political stratification and argued that 'the intercorrelation among the three forms of stratification is far from being perfect' (1964: 12). Yet, he did not cite Weber's contribution to social stratification, but he referred to Marx's theory of class and social change and rejected it at an early stage of his analysis. He claimed on the basis of empirical data from America and England, plus several other societies, that as far as Marx's polarization and proletarianization theses were concerned, 'practically all his predictions have failed' (1964: 45). However, in addition to claiming that Marx's increased economic differentiation hypothesis was 'fallacious', Sorokin also rejected the opposite view, namely that there is 'a marked and consistent tendency of economic equalization' (1964: 45). He argued that 'if economic stratification has not increased, at any rate, it has not decreased either', and therefore he supported 'the theory of trendless fluctuation' (1964: 46). Sorokin was unconvinced by the assumption that 'vertical social mobility at the present time is much greater than in the past . . . is a mere belief which has not been tested as yet' (1964: 154–5).

In the absence of any large-scale surveys of mobility, Sorokin's method was to review the many small-scale studies then available, which he supplemented with his own data on different social groups in Minneapolis. Among his numerous specific conclusions, he first asserted that although family background was still a factor in social placement, education was becoming more important as the social function of the school changed from that of an educational institution to a 'testing, selecting, and distributing agency' (1964: 188).

Second, although Sorokin found evidence of considerable occupational inheritance or stability, he argued that:

Within present Western societies the transmission of occupational status seems to be in all occupational groups much less than 100 per cent; its maximum seems to be at about 70 per cent; its minimum at about 3 to 10 per cent.

(1964: 419).

Sorokin calculated that the average father-son transmission of occupation fluctuated between 20 and 60 per cent, thus implying that it varies considerably from one occupation to another.

Third, Sorokin suggested 'a definite trend of a decrease of inheritance of occupational status', albeit cautiously in view of the paucity of data, the emphasis on the historically declining farm population, and the contrary evidence provided by his study of American millionaires (1964: 424).

Fourth, in view of the volume of vertical male inter- and intra-occupational mobility current in western societies, Sorokin concluded that: 'The picture given by some countries varies somewhat in detail, but in essence it is similar to that of the United States of America' (1964: 443). This key point contradicts Sombart's view (discussed in Chapter 4) that America has a distinctively high rate of social mobility.

Fifth, with reference to the politics of mobility, Sorokin argued that, since occupational inheritance was the most common pattern, 'the partisans of the class struggle may have a reason for their theory and aspirations' (1964: 439). Yet Sorokin also noted that 'it is not accurate to depict present economic classes as "hereditarily rich" or "hereditarily poor" ' because class composition is 'fluid, changeable, and unstable, at least in part' (1964: 478). Thus, Sorokin judged that mobility can promote social stability as it 'robs the revolutionary factions of their possible and capable leaders' (1964: 533–4), but it can also undermine social order as 'individuals, groups and factions of a mobile society' fight to achieve upward mobility (1964: 535). Moreover, he argued that in a crisis, the 'suffering masses do not accept their situation' and may turn to violence and revolution 'when legal forms of fight fail' (1964: 535). In this respect, Sorokin anticipated Merton's analysis of the use of illegitimate means to achieve legitimate cultural goals, which was central to the latter's theory of deviance (1968). This is not surprising since Sorokin founded the sociology department at Harvard University and Merton studied under him at the same institution (Allen 1963; Coser 1977).

Thus, Sorokin's wide-ranging and pioneering sociological study of mobility was more neo-Weberian than neo-Marxist in that he regarded modern societies as inherently mobile and hence 'efficient' (1964: 532). However, he acknowledged the possibility of revolution due to the 'explosive' combination of a 'degenerated aristocracy' with 'hereditary proletarians' pushing from below (Sorokin 1964: 372 and 439).

It is important to note that when Sorokin referred to individuals he meant males, as can be seen from all his key tables and detailed sub-headings (e.g. Chapter XVII). Women are only mentioned briefly in the context of marital mobility (1964: 179). Hence, Sorokin conforms to the generalization that, with the notable exception of Veblen (Edgell 1987), early American sociologists were 'sexists to a man' (Schwendinger and Schwendinger 1971: 783). If Sorokin's study had been almost exclusively about female mobility rather than male mobility, no doubt the title of his book would have reflected this fact.

Sexism in sociology has only recently been challenged, but not much has changed (Abbott and Wallace 1990). Virtually the only sociological specialism in which women are more prominent than men is family sociology, which amounts to 'reverse sexism and has been called more accurately wives' family sociology' (Safilious-Rothschild 1969). As will become apparent below, all the major post-Sorokin American and British mobility studies have concentrated on male mobility, though typically this is not made clear in the title of the studies (see for example, Blau and Duncan 1967; Glass 1964). Thus, of necessity, male and female mobility will be considered separately.

CONTEMPORARY MALE SOCIAL MOBILITY

In post-1945 Anglo-American sociology, the first major cross-national study of social mobility was produced in America and combined a secondary analysis of cross-national data with an empirical survey of mobility in Oakland, California (Lipset and Bendix 1959). On the basis of an analysis of national surveys, including those undertaken by Rogoff in the United States (1953) and by Glass in Britain (1964), Lipset and Bendix argued that industrialization leads to high mobility rates and concluded that 'the overall pattern of social mobility appears to be the same in the industrial societies of various Western countries' (1959: 13). This has since become known as the Lipset-Zetterberg (or LZ) thesis (Zetterberg was the co-author of the first paper that advanced this generalization, see Lipset and Zetterberg 1956).

The thesis was based on absolute vertical mobility rates of males across the manual/non-manual line, and it contrasts with Sorokin's cautiousness regarding historical mobility trends. However, in certain other respects, Lipset and Bendix's mobility research was very much in the Sorokin tradition – for example, in its emphasis on the selection function of education and the adoption of a multidimensional approach to stratification.

A notable discontinuity between the Sorokin and the Lipset and Bendix studies is that the latter concentrated on the movement from manual to non-manual occupations, which they defined as upward mobility, despite expressing a number of reservations about this distinction. At the beginning of their study they admitted that: 'It is true, of course, that many white-collar positions are lower in income and prestige than higher levels of skilled manual work' (Lipset and Bendix 1959: 16). But they went on to justify their emphasis on this cleavage by noting that 'most of these poorly paid white-collar positions are held by women, and male white-collar workers are often able to secure higher-level supervisory posts' (Lipset and Bendix 1959: 16). This line of argument has since become a major debating point in the sociology of class, as we have seen already (see Chapter 4). A related point is that Lipset and Bendix recognized that their use of the manual/non-manual distinction in a comparative study of mobility involved the problematic assumption that there is 'consensus on the relative status of different occupations' (1959: 269). Moreover, they conceded that 'it obscures such significant shifts as those involved in movements from a skilled manual occupation to a low-level white-collar position, or from either of these to modest self-employment' (Lipset and Bendix 1959: 270). Lipset and Bendix defended their assumption that 'a move from manual to non-manual employment constitutes upward mobility among males' on five grounds: prestige, income, education, subjective middle class/consumption and political attitudes (1959: 15–16). However, in a revealing comment at the end of their study they noted that: 'This approach to occupational classification is theoretically neat and operationally easy' (Lipset and Bendix 1959: 270).

Since this famous study of male mobility there have been two reviews of the literature, by Miller (1960) and Heath (1981), using data of 'limited' comparability (Erikson and Goldthorpe 1992: 27), surveys of mobility in America (Blau and Duncan 1967; Hauser and Featherman 1977; Featherman and Hauser

1978), and Britain (Goldthorpe 1987) which focus on male mobility, and an international study of male and female mobility (Erikson and Goldthorpe 1992).

Miller (1960) compared the male mobility data for eighteen nations including Britain and America, and distinguished between mass mobility and movement into elite positions from various subordinate classes. He found that mass mobility from manual to non-manual occupations varied from under 10 per cent to over 30 per cent with both Britain (25 per cent) and the USA (29 per cent) in the high upward mobility group of nations. In terms of elite mobility, Miller found that the USA, at 28 per cent, had the highest rate of movement into the elite of all the nations examined except the Soviet Union, which can be regarded as problematic on the grounds of the old (1940) and unusual (emigrant) data for this country. Miller's analysis of cross-national male mobility rates contradicted the LZ thesis with respect to the unusually high rate of elite mobility in the USA, thereby confirming Sombart's hypothesis of American exceptionalism. In the case of manual to non-manual movement, Miller's analysis failed to support the LZ thesis regarding the basic similarity of male social mobility in industrial societies, but the USA was not distinctively high in terms of this measure. Thus, Miller failed to confirm the more general version of Sombart's American exceptionalism theory. In other words, by distinguishing between mass and elite mobility, Miller was able to show that the USA was unexceptional with regard to the former and exceptional with regard to the latter, and that both types of mobility varied from one country to another.

The Blau and Duncan study was undertaken in 1962 and involved a representative sample of over 20,000 men. It was primarily concerned with mobility in America, but included a discussion of mobility rates in different societies. Although Blau and Duncan mention Marx on economic class and Weber on the distinction between class position and prestige status, their reformulation of the issue of social mobility in contemporary societies draws upon American functionalist theory, which assigns a central place to the occupational structure and to the achievement of status within it. They started from the assumption that 'the understanding of social stratification in modern society is best promoted by the systematic investigation of occupational status and mobility' (1967: 5). They justified their approach by claiming, without deeming it necessary to provide any empirical evidence, that Marx's conceptualization of class 'is no longer adequate for differentiating . . . men in control of the large capitalistic enterprises from those subject to their control, because controlling managers of the largest concerns today are themselves employees of corporations' (1967: 6).

Blau and Duncan defined class as 'the role persons occupy in the economy and their managerial influence on economic concerns', and this enabled them to argue that: 'Occupational position does not encompass all aspects of the concept of class, but it is probably the best single indicator of it' (1967: 6). They further claimed that following from their emphasis on the occupational dimension of class, occupational position is closer conceptually to economic class than prestige status. In the light of this argument, Blau and Duncan asserted that the occupational structure is the 'foundation for the main dimensions of social stratification' (1967: 6).

The aim of Blau and Duncan's research was to specify the variables that influence individual occupational achievement. Concerning the 'relative importance' of ascription and achievement, they stated that: 'In a liberal democratic society we think of the more basic principle as being that of achievement. Some ascriptive features of the system may be regarded as vestiges of an earlier epoch, to be extirpated as readily as possible' (1967: 163). Thus, their study was based on two related and equally suspect assumptions: that the ownership of property is no longer crucial to the class analysis of modern societies, and that in such societies the achievement principle prevails.

Strictly speaking, therefore, the Blau and Duncan study is not about class mobility in either the Marxist or Weberian sense (for a neo-Marxist critique see Crowder 1974, and for a neo-Weberian critique see Goldthorpe 1987), but is concerned with the attainment of occupational status in the context of a functionalist theoretical framework (for a critique of this distinctly American approach to social stratification see Huaco 1966). However, since they question the LZ thesis that modern societies have similar rates of social mobility and discuss historical trends, it is necessary to consider their contribution to the debate about contemporary male mobility.

Blau and Duncan listed four criticisms of the LZ thesis:

1 the unreliability of the LZ data;

2 the advanced state of industrialization and education in America;

3 the minimal status distinctions in America compared to Europe and Japan; and

4 the need to take into account access to elite status in addition to movement across the blue/white-collar divide.

In the light of these points, Blau and Duncan suggest that: 'The prevailing impression that chances of social mobility are superior in the United States should not be dismissed out of hand' (1967: 432). On the basis of their American survey and other cross-national data, including Miller's (1960), they confirmed that there was little difference among various industrial societies in the rate of mobility between blue- and white-collar occupations. However, and more importantly, they claimed, like Miller, that elite mobility in America was exceptionally high and speculated that this was due to the 'high level of popular education in the United States, perhaps reinforced by the lesser emphasis on formal distinctions of social status' (Blau and Duncan 1967: 435). Yet they also noted that most men in America do not attain high occupational status, but do experience an improvement in their standard of living and hence their social status via 'conspicuous consumption' (Blau and Duncan 1967: 338; for a discussion of this term, see Edgell and Tilman 1991). Finally, they noted that:

> The stability of American democracy is undoubtedly related to the superior chances of upward mobility in this country, its high standard of living, and the low degree of status deference between social strata. For these conditions make it unlikely that large numbers of underprivileged men experience oppression, despair of all hope, and become so disaffected with the existing system of differential rewards as well as with political institutions that they join extremist political movements committed to violent rebellion.
>
> (Blau and Duncan 1967: 439).

Aside from its vastly more sophisticated and innovative methodology, notably its theoretically informed use of path analysis (for an appraisal of this aspect of the study see Featherman 1981), Blau and Duncan's research can be located in the Sorokin sociology of mobility tradition. Both studies focused on male inter- and intra-generational occupational mobility and the relative influence of ascription and achievement on occupational attainment. However, Blau and Duncan were more confident than both Sorokin, and Lipset and Bendix, regarding the trend toward universalism, but parted company with both of these earlier studies in respect of Sombart's thesis of American exceptionalism. In other words, Blau and Duncan confirmed the LZ thesis with reference to the similar cross-national pattern of manual to non-manual mobility, and confirmed the Sombart thesis with reference to the distinctively high rate of elite mobility in the USA. Thus, with their emphasis on long-range upward mobility and the role of conspicuous consumption, Blau and Duncan's study of mobility represents a modern version of Sombart's 'roast beef and apple pie' theory of social stability (see Chapter 4).

Blau and Duncan's male mobility in America research has been re-analysed (Hauser and Featherman 1977) and, more unusually, replicated with an even larger sample of over 33,000 males (Featherman and Hauser 1978). In the process of re-analysing Blau and Duncan's 1962 data, Featherman and Hauser, plus Jones, acknowledged Miller's qualification of the LZ hypothesis and reformulated their thesis on the basis of distinguishing between 'observed' or absolute mobility and 'circulation' or relative mobility in their comparative study of American and Australian male mobility (Hauser and Featherman 1977: 15). They claimed that 'industrial societies can be shown not to have the same rates of observed mobility', but 'that once structural mobility has been taken into account [i.e. occupational opportunity structures for fathers and sons], circulation mobility has been nearly constant over time' (1977: 15). This constant relative mobility thesis has since become known as the FJH thesis.

Featherman and Hauser's (1978) replication of Blau and Duncan's study found little change from 1962 to 1973 in the rate of inter-generational occupational mobility, but an increase in the rate of intra-generational mobility. They also found great immobility at the extremes of the occupational hierarchy and considerable mobility in the middle. They noted that: 'Both within and between generations, occupational mobility chances have remained remarkably constant over the historical periods covered' (Featherman and Hauser 1978: 216).

Thus, in their detailed replication study, Featherman and Hauser found evidence of change as well as stability, and this mixed picture led them to be reluctant to make any sweeping statements. Hence it was only in the context of extensive qualification with reference to the labour market that they claimed to have 'detected two complementary trends: declining status ascription and increasingly universalistic status allocation' (1978: 481). Thus Featherman and Hauser's replication study confirmed Blau and Duncan's finding of a high rate of social mobility in America and their 'fundamental trend' towards universalism, but ended on a cautionary note: 'The future course of mobility in the United States is not inevitable, our national ideology notwithstanding' (1978: 495)

The issue of cross-national variations in male social mobility, and by implication the question of American exceptionalism, was reviewed by Heath (1981) with reference to surveys conducted between 1963 and 1974 in nineteen industrial societies. Heath confirmed the existence of considerable variation in terms of both mass and elite, absolute and relative mobility rates, with the USA high on each count but not exceptionally so. Heath's analysis contradicted all the social mobility theories discussed in this section, namely Sombart's thesis of American exceptionalism, the LZ thesis of cross-national similarity in mobility rates (including the Miller/Blau and Duncan variation concerning the distinctiveness of elite mobility in America), and the FJH hypothesis regarding the constancy of relative mobility. However, this did not lead Heath to reiterate Sorokin's theory of trendless variations. Instead, he suggested that national variations were related to the economic and political development of different types of society, such as 'new' and 'old', and socialist and conservative (Heath 1981: 222–3).

The large-scale study of male mobility in Britain undertaken by Goldthorpe in 1972, and updated in 1983, was interested in mobility 'from the standpoint of its implications for class formation and class action', and therefore adopted a class rather than a status model of society (1987: 28). In this respect, Goldthorpe noted that his study had more in common with the original debate with Marx, exemplified by the work of Sorokin, than with the Blau and Duncan project. Goldthorpe used the terms upward and downward mobility to refer solely to movement into and out of classes I and II, that is his 'service class' and the 'cadet levels of the service class' (1987: 41 and 43). His aim was to address three class-mobility theses:

> That of a marked degree of "closure" existing at the higher levels of the class structure; that of a "buffer

zone" restricting the extent of mobility across the division between manual and nonmanual occupations; and that of the offsetting or "counterbalancing" of any rising trend in upward mobility intergenerationally by a declining trend in such mobility intragenerationally.

(Goldthorpe 1987: 40)

Goldthorpe's analysis of his absolute mobility data amounted to a qualified refutation of all three theses. First, the closure thesis was rejected on the evidence of 'a very wide basis of recruitment and a very low degree of homogeneity' in class I, although 'far greater homogeneity in terms of social origins' was found at the other end of the class structure (1987: 44). Second, there was some evidence of long-range upward and downward mobility and short-range mobility across the manual/non-manual divide which contradicted the buffer zone thesis. Goldthorpe also reported 'marked inequalities in mobility chances to the disadvantage of men of working-class background' (1987: 50). Third, it was noted that,

while our findings could perhaps be taken as lending support to the claim that mobility chances are becoming increasingly influenced by educational attainments, they go contrary to the counterbalance thesis in indicating that, over recent decades, an increase in direct entry to the higher levels of the class structure has occurred without there being any apparent decline in the chances of access via indirect routes.

(Goldthorpe 1987: 58).

However, Goldthorpe proceeded to suggest that as far as male mobility in Britain was concerned, 'the closure, buffer zone and counterbalance theses would all have much more to commend them if reformulated so as to refer to relative, rather than to absolute mobility rates' or social fluidity (1987: 121). Social fluidity refers to the degree of openness in a society 'in the sense of how equal are chances of access to different class situations for individuals for different class origins' (Goldthorpe 1987: 305). According to Goldthorpe, the issue of class formation is best considered using absolute mobility data, whereas the issue of openness is best considered using relative mobility data. Goldthorpe found that there had been an increase in the rate of absolute mobility, but no improvement in relative mobility chances. Thus, although the chances of being upwardly mobile had improved, the relative mobility chances of people from different classes had remained the same.

Goldthorpe updated his study eleven years later and found no change in the rate of relative mobility but a slight increase in absolute mobility. He found that 'the return of mass unemployment has created a serious risk of what can only be regarded as downward mobility – and that the risk is much greater for men in working class positions' (1987: 269).

Goldthorpe also considered male mobility in contemporary Britain in relation to cross-national theories and data. He noted that the first comparative mobility thesis advanced by Lipset and Zetterberg (LZ thesis) had been superseded by the FJH hypothesis. He distinguished between a 'strict' and a 'less strict' interpretation of the FJH hypothesis and suggested that the latter was more 'sustainable' than the former to the extent that it refers to a broad rather than a 'complete uniformity in cross-cultural patterns of social fluidity' or relative mobility (Goldthorpe 1987: 303). On the basis of comparative data from nine countries, including England and Wales, and the USA, he confirmed the validity of the 'similar relative-dissimilar absolute' FJH mobility hypothesis, and concluded that 'cross-national variation in absolute mobility rates is largely the result of structural differences' (Goldthorpe 1987: 322)

In his own work, and in collaboration with other social mobility researchers, Goldthorpe has examined international variations in male mobility with reference to convergence theory and American exceptionalism (Erikson, Goldthorpe and Portocarero 1979; 1982; 1983; Erikson and Goldthorpe 1985; Goldthorpe 1987). These studies provided little supporting evidence for either view. Regarding the former theory, it was found that specific convergent tendencies, such as those associated with the growth of the service class, vary in different societies (Goldthorpe 1987). Significantly, it has been suggested that cross-national variations in absolute mobility rates 'might well be taken as supporting Sorokin's thesis of trendless fluctuation' (Erikson, Goldthorpe and Portocarero 1983: 340). Regarding the alleged exceptional rate of upward mobility in America, Erikson and Goldthorpe (1985) have reviewed the mobility evidence in the light of a complex recoding of English data to make it comparable with American data, namely the 1973 data used by Featherman and Hauser (1978) to replicate the study by Blau and Duncan (1967).

Despite distinguishing between absolute and relative mobility, as well as between manual and non-manual and elite social mobility, in an attempt to do justice to the complexity of the topic, they found that 'the USA does not have exceptionally high rates of social mobility' (Erikson and Goldthorpe 1985: 20). Thus, Erikson and Goldthorpe's findings failed to confirm either Sombart's thesis regarding American exceptionalism or the LZ thesis regarding the basic similarity of international absolute mobility rates.

Goldthorpe's discussion of the class implications of his findings on male mobility concentrated on the degree of openness of the British class system and on class formation with special reference to the service class and the working class. Regarding the first issue, he claimed on the basis of his relative mobility data that in post-war Britain, 'no significant reduction in class inequalities was in fact achieved' (Goldthorpe 1987: 328). This was despite economic growth and a political strategy of egalitarian reform aimed at reducing social inequality. He concluded that 'this strategy grossly misjudges the resistance that the class structure can offer to attempts to change it' (1987: 328). (This point is reminiscent of Vanneman and Cannon's (1987) claim, discussed in Chapter 4, that in America the ability of the dominant capitalist class to maintain the status quo exceeds that of the subordinates class to change it.) Goldthorpe added that economic growth and the increase in absolute mobility had 'served effectively to distract attention away from the issue of whether at the same time any equalization of relative mobility chances was being achieved' (1987: 328–9).

Regarding the issue of class formation, Goldthorpe argued that evidence on trends in absolute mobility rates indicated that the service class had a 'low degree of demographic identity', in contrast to the working class, which was 'more homogeneous . . . so far as the social origins of their members are concerned' (1987: 332 and 336). However, he also noted that during the recessionary 1980s in Britain, the 'polarization of working-class mobility chances' could lead to the emergence of an underclass within the working class (Goldthorpe 1987: 337). Goldthorpe also judged that the extensive upward mobility into the service class tended to 'favour integration and stability rather than discontent and an impetus to change', since the upwardly mobile generally approved of the existing social order in which they had been successful (1987: 340). However, he qualified this conclusion by noting that sectoral divisions within the service class were a source of potential political diversity. Whilst some research in Britain has confirmed that Goldthorpe was correct to anticipate this possibility (Dunleavy and Husbands 1985; Edgell and Duke 1991), evidence also exists that contradicts the sectoral cleavage theory (Marshall *et al.* 1988).

If upward mobility stabilizes society, does a lack of it have a destabilizing effect? Goldthorpe found 'little resentment' among the small number of men who had been downwardly mobile or among those who had been stable within the working class (1987: 342). He suggested that the main reason for this was the 'low social visibility' of the relative mobility rate trend, and the 'high social visibility' of the 'actual extent of upward mobility' (1987: 342). Thus, the immobile are not only likely to know of someone who had been upwardly mobile, but also be better off as a result of economic development, yet be far less aware of macro social trends.

There are two main lines of criticism of Goldthorpe's approach to social mobility. The first concerns his concentration on male mobility and the second involves his use of the distinction between absolute and relative mobility. Both have been contested by Goldthorpe and will be considered in the context of the next two sections.

CONTEMPORARY FEMALE SOCIAL MOBILITY

Sorokin's study is known as 'the first comprehensive treatise on social mobility' (Erikson and Goldthorpe 1985: 2), but to the extent that it focused on male mobility, this judgement is questionable. It was the first comprehensive study of male social mobility. Until recently, studies of social mobility seem to have taken their cue from Sorokin. Glass (1954), Lipset and Bendix (1959), Blau and Duncan (1967), Featherman and Hauser (1978) and Goldthorpe (1987) all concentrated on male mobility.

Although Glass collected some female mobility data in 1949, it was not analysed for ten years (Kelsall and Mitchell 1959). Lipset and Bendix's Oakland study included a small percentage of women in their capacity as 'heads of households', but excluded female respondents from many of their tables. They justified their exclusion of female mobility on pragmatic grounds; 'meaningful comparisons of the occupational status of fathers and daughters is much more difficult than comparisons of fathers and sons'

(Lipset and Bendix 1959: 151). Blau and Duncan collected some data on their male respondents' wives and mothers, but limited their study to men as a 'legitimate preliminary simplification', yet admitted that 'the supply of openings available to men can hardly be independent of the number of women ready and trained to work at a variety of skill levels' (1967: 113; see also Featherman and Hauser 1978: 493). Goldthorpe included material on female mobility in the second but not the first edition of his study, on the grounds of economy (1987/1980). Prior to discussing the current pattern of female mobility, it is instructive to consider the possible reasons why the female half of society made up about 1 per cent of mobility research until recently (Glenn *et al*. 1974).

In the 1920s, sexism was rife in society and sociology; women were ghettoized in the family and in family sociology. Arguably, Sorokin could therefore be forgiven for neglecting to examine female mobility. However, the advancement of women during this century has rendered this excuse progressively less convincing. The first critique of sexist class analysis was directed at American sociology, especially functionalist theories of stratification (Watson and Barth 1964). It was argued that 'the patriarchal family model with husband working full time at an occupation, which underlies much of stratification theory, is not an adequate model of contemporary society' (Watson and Barth 1964: 13). Acker (1973) cited Watson and Barth's critique of sexist stratification research but also pointed out that the minority status of women had been discussed in a US sociology journal in the early 1950s (Hacker 1951), and even earlier in the appendix of a major book on American society (Myrdal 1944). Thus, in the second half of this century, there would seem to be no excuse for neglecting women if the object of one's study is the whole class structure.

Goldthorpe's defence of the decision to focus on male mobility in his first national study has been described in terms of making a 'virtue' of 'expediency' (Dex 1987: 24). In other words, initially it was justified on the pragmatic basis of economy, and later on the grounds of scepticism regarding the alleged negative consequences of excluding women for our comprehension of mobility. The debate about women and mobility research is part of the problem of 'integrating women into class theory' (Dale *et al*. 1985: 384) that has been discussed already (see Chapter 3). When Goldthorpe belatedly included women in his account of mobility in Britain he confirmed his suspicion that to exclude them does not, for the most part, produce a distorted picture of the class structure.

Goldthorpe examined the class mobility of women using three quite different units of class analysis and discovered that it is only when the individual approach is adopted, rather than the conventional or dominance approaches, that differences in the absolute mobility rates of men and women are revealed, notably the more frequent downward mobility of women. Thus, in this respect it could be argued that 'our understanding of mobility within the British class structure is grossly impaired by studies which have concentrated on the experience of men' (Goldthorpe 1987: 295; Goldthorpe and Payne 1986: 549).

The debate about women and class has been summarized, criticized and evaluated comprehensively by Marshall *et al.* (1988). They noted that it involves two linked issues, the 'scope' and unit of class analysis. They found that in terms of absolute mobility, men are more likely to experience upward mobility than women, especially into the service class, and that this was not unrelated to the greater domestic role responsibilities of women. They concluded that as far as the scope of class analysis is concerned, since male and female mobility experiences are different yet interdependent, women should not be excluded from class analysis. Thus, the focus on male mobility 'generates a misleading "map" of the class structure' (Marshall *et al.* 1988: 112). Regarding the unit of class analysis issue, they argued that much depends upon one's research objectives, and commented that Goldthorpe's preference for the family unit was 'consistent with his conception of class analysis' (Marshall *et al.* 1988: 85). However, they criticized his perspective for not being broad enough to recognize that the class structure is gendered, and concluded that: 'Social classes comprise neither families nor individuals but individuals in families' (Marshall *et al.* 1988: 85). In other words, men and women should be allocated to a class on the basis of their own occupations, since sexual segregation prevails in the labour market and this is reflected in the contrasting class distribution of men and women and the associated variation in their absolute mobility rates.

Support for this view has been reported by Payne and Abbott (1990), who found that men were more likely to be upwardly mobile than women, whereas women were more likely to be downwardly mobile than men. They too concluded that the full development of class theory requires the inclusion of 'men and women into our research' (Payne and Abbott 1990: 174). In the same volume, Abbott (1990; see also Abbott and Sapsford 1987) has reported her re-examination of Goldthorpe's male-based account of the closure, buffer zone and counterbalancing theses using female data. She found that the top of the class structure was more closed for women than men, that a buffer zone operates at the manual/non-manual work divide in the case of women, and that upon entry to the labour market, women were less likely than men to experience upward mobility. Thus, in contrast to Goldthorpe, Abbott's female mobility data supported all three theses, and she therefore concluded that 'an analysis of male occupational mobility by itself gives an inadequate picture of the nature of contemporary British society' (Abbott 1990: 44).

Goldthorpe has since examined systematically with cross-national data the argument that studies of male mobility are 'misleading' (Erikson and Goldthorpe 1992: 265). On the basis of 'complete' mobility tables, and using the dominance method to determine family class, it was found that women's experience of class mobility differed very little from that of men. Hence, there was no need to revise his earlier conclusions. Yet when an individual unit of class analysis is used, 'women's absolute – though not relative – rates of class mobility . . . diverge appreciably from those of men' (Erikson and Goldthorpe 1992: 275). However, this approach is considered 'invalid' for basically the same reasons that he advocated a family unit of analysis in the first place (see Chapter 3 and Erikson and Goldthorpe 1992: 235–8).

SUMMARY AND CONCLUSIONS

Sociological research on social mobility affords an excellent example of the cumulative nature of Anglo-American social scientific knowledge (Featherman 1981). Concepts and theories dating from the work of Sombart and Sorokin at the beginning of the twentieth century have been progressively developed in the light of new findings, and in the process, statistical techniques of data analysis have been transformed. For example, the LZ thesis has been superseded by the FJH hypothesis, and basic percentages have been replaced by odds ratios (for a guide to statistical terms used in mobility research see Heath 1981 Appendix II). One of the by-products of successive conceptual, theoretical and methodological refinements has been an increase in complexity that defies neat and easy generalization. Further, it seems that social mobility is a topic which encourages highly technical quantification, and which has tended to result in the confirmation of the findings of earlier, less sophisticated studies.

This is readily apparent from the most recent and comprehensive research report of cross-national mobility (Erikson and Goldthorpe 1992). This study focuses on rates and patterns of mobility over time as well as space and includes data on no less than twelve countries including America, England and Wales, Scotland, and Northern Ireland. The main results of this study tended to confirm earlier research, notably trendlessness in the pattern of absolute mobility, stability in the pattern of relative mobility, and minimal mobility evidence in support of the thesis of American exceptionalism. In other words, after over half a century of research involving considerable theoretical and methodological progress, there is now massive, though refined, support for Sorokin and the FJH hypothesis, and partial rejection of Sombart.

At the centre of many of the debates about social mobility is the distinction between absolute and relative mobility. It will be recalled that Goldthorpe argued that the former, actual observable mobility is relevant to the analysis of class formation, whereas the latter, the relative chances of people from different social backgrounds achieving upward mobility, is related to the issue of openness. Payne (1990) and Saunders (1990) have argued that Goldthorpe's emphasis on unchanging relative mobility rates, rather than on increasing absolute mobility rates, gives the false impression that Britain is still a less than open society. Goldthorpe has responded to this line of criticism by emphasizing the distinction between absolute and relative mobility and reiterating that 'during the present century Britain may have become a somewhat more mobile society, as a result of structural change, it has not become a more fluid or more open one' (Goldthorpe 1990: 422). Thus, according to Goldthorpe, it is not a matter of general impressions, but of making important distinctions, notably between different rates of mobility, and of resisting simple conclusions.

Finally, in the recessionary 1990s, mass bankruptcies, mass unemployment, and the growth of what has been called 'non-standard (paid) work' – for example, part-time and temporary labour contracts (Fevre 1991: 56) – may well provide future mobility researchers with findings which raise doubts about the generalization that during this century, upward mobility is more common than downward mobility in modern societies.

6

Class, inequality and politics

INTRODUCTION

In the classic sociological theories of Marx and Weber, class was accorded a central theme by virtue of its pivotal role in structuring inequality and politics. For Marx the creation and distribution of wealth and income are an expression of the system of production, characterized in the case of capitalism by workers who receive wages and owners who receive profits. Furthermore, Marx argued that: 'Political power, properly so called, is merely the organised power of one class for oppressing another' (Marx and Engels 1848: 90). Although Weber also argued that class was fundamental to the distribution of economic power, he differed from Marx in suggesting that at the political level, 'parties may represent interests determined through "class situation" or "status situation", and they may recruit their following respectively from one or the other' (1961: 194). In modern parlance, if you want to know about the distribution of wealth or political attitudes and behaviour, and much else besides, such as the patterning of health and illness, the consumption of goods and services, or educational achievement (Reid 1989), class analysis is essential.

In this chapter, the sociological significance of the concept of class will be demonstrated in two ways: first with reference to what Westergaard and Resler have called 'the hard core of class', namely economic inequality (1975: 2); and second with reference to class and voting behaviour.

CLASS AND ECONOMIC INEQUALITY: MEASUREMENT PROBLEMS

The sociological analysis of the relationship between class and economic inequality is fraught with difficulties, most of which can be understood with reference to the three choices faced by researchers concerned with operationalizing class, namely conceptual scheme, unit of analysis and degree of coverage (see also Chapter 3).

Conceptual scheme

Both Marx and Weber regarded the ownership of property and propertylessness as the 'basic categories of all class situations' (Weber 1961: 182), and this formed the essential part of their respective class schemes. Yet economic inequality data rarely if ever match their class categories and concentrate instead on either the distribution of wealth (i.e. broadly equivalent to the ownership capital) or of income (i.e. broadly equivalent to the selling of labour power). This has led to a tradition of two main ways of presenting economic inequality data. The first is to show the percentage share of total wealth (and sometimes income) received by different proportions of the adult population, and the second is to show the value of the income (often including 'unearned' income) of different occupational groups. The net result is that data are available on the extent of the concentration of wealth at the 'top' of society and it can reasonably be assumed that the richest people in society are the owners of capital, not the sellers of labour power. Data are also available on the patterning of occupational class income inequalities, typically divided into the familiar atheoretical and empirically problematic non-manual and manual categories. What is lacking is comprehensive data on the distribution of wealth *and* income for social *and* occupational classes.

Unit of analysis

The family is often taken as the unit of class analysis for the purpose of measuring economic inequality. This approach assumes that all family members share equally the total income, but if this does not occur, the family unit of analysis would be an inaccurate measure of class inequality, in which case it may be better to use the individual as the unit of class analysis. Research in Britain has shown that a wife's share of household income tends to be higher if she participates in the labour market (Piachaud 1982), and that a pooling system in which both partners have access to household income is more common among younger than older couples (Pahl 1989). This suggests that although the family unit of analysis may conceal the extent of financial inequality within families, since all members of a family share to a greater or lesser extent total household income, the family is probably the appropriate unit of class analysis in an investigation of the patterning of economic inequality. Arguably, the optimum strategy would be to collect and present data on both the individual and family/household bases. As ever, much depends upon the purpose(s) of the research and practical considerations such as the knowledge and cooperativeness of respondents.

Degree of coverage

Traditionally, in class analysis, only the economically active are included. However, this approach typically excludes the exceptionally wealthy 'leisure class' (Veblen 1970) and the exceptionally poor underclass (Heisler 1991), which in the case of a study of the patterning of class inequality would constitute two significant omissions. Hence, for a complete picture of class inequality, all adults should be included.

There is an additional dimension to the degree of coverage in the study of the class distribution of wealth and income, and that concerns the time-scale of one's measure. The basic choice involves the distinction between a person's current income, measured over a week, month or year, and a lifetime measure (Atkinson 1974). The two measures will produce vastly different results because over the life-cycle individuals typically experience variations in income (Atkinson 1983). This is, in part, another way of saying that an individual's class situation can change over time, for example, due to upward and downward social mobility. But it is also a matter of income variations within any one class situation, for example, as a result of overtime or short-time in the case of manual workers and salary increments or promotion in the case of professional workers. There is also the possibility of the inheritance of wealth that could transform a penurious student into a millionaire. Thus, the longer the time-scale, the fuller the account of the patterning of economic inequality.

There is one further difficulty associated with the investigation of economic inequality, and that concerns the accuracy of the data however the concept class is operationalized. The unreliability of official statistics in general (Hindess 1973; Irvine *et al.* 1979), and specifically with reference to the distribution of wealth and income (Atkinson 1983; Hird and Irvine 1979; Johnson 1973; Kolko 1962; Levy 1987; Titmuss 1962), is legendary. For example, state accountants are concerned to ensure that all those liable to pay taxes pay them and only those eligible for state benefits receive them. Consequently, income and wealth surveys are faced with the problem that it is in the interests of people to underestate their wealth and income in order to pay less tax and/or receive more benefits. There is of course no way of knowing precisely the extent of this problem. But what can be stated with confidence is that surveys of the poor are far more common than surveys of the rich, and the rich are more capable of defending themselves against inquisitive state accountants than the poor. Furthermore, the sums involved in so-called 'welfare scrounging' are probably far smaller than the amounts involved in tax evasion, legitimate and otherwise. Hence the claim by Miliband that: 'State taxes and benefits are an intrinsic part of the [unequal] class struggle' (1989: 139). Thus, statistics on class and economic inequality should be interpreted with extreme caution.

Finally, the terms wealth and income have been and will be used in the usual way to refer to the ownership of capital, e.g. land, buildings, stocks and shares, which can be sold, and income, both earned and unearned, e.g. wages and interest.

CLASS AND ECONOMIC INEQUALITY: DATA

With these numerous but not insurmountable difficulties in mind, it is now possible to consider the issue of class and economic inequality in contemporary Britain and America. In order to do so, we can start, yet again, with Marx, and his famous immiseration thesis. Marx claimed that it was a law of capitalist development that the 'accumulation of wealth' at the top of society was related to the 'accumulation of misery' at the bottom of society (1970a: 645). In other words, poverty is the source of wealth in a capitalist society. Thus, Marx envisaged the growth of an increasingly wealthy capitalist class and an increasingly poor working class, but noted of this generalization: 'Like all other laws it is modified in its working by many circumstances' (1970a: 644). Marx's increasingly relative immiseration thesis was an integral part of his proletarianization theory of class development discussed above (see Chapters 1 and 4). In order to examine the claim that capitalist 'progress' involves widening class inequality, data on the percentage shares of total wealth and the occupational class pattern of income inequality will be presented.

Regarding the first type of data, assuming that the richest 5 per cent of the adult population of Britain (used loosely since the 1950–72 data refer to Great Britain, and the 1976–88 data to the United Kingdom), are broadly the equivalent of the capitalist class, since the end of the Second World War there has been a decline in the share of wealth owned by those at the top of the class structure, from over 70 to about 50 per cent (Atkinson 1980; Social Trends 1991). Taking a more short-term view, this trend seems to have been halted, even reversed, during the Thatcher era of regressive taxation (Riddell 1989; Stark 1987). A similar though less pronounced historical trend is apparent for the USA (Smith and Franklin 1980), and for the Reagan era (Cohen and Rodgers 1988; Winnick 1989). Thus, in both Britain and the USA the distribution of wealth became less concentrated in the post-war era, a time of state intervention in the economy, but more concentrated in the 1980s.

At the other end of the class structure poverty has persisted in the most economically advanced societies (for the UK see Townsend 1979 and for the USA see Harrington 1984). More specifically, between 1945 and 1979, the share of total income before tax received by the least affluent (the bottom 30 per cent in the UK and the bottom 20 per cent in the USA) has remained constant at around 10 per cent in the UK and under 4 per cent in the USA (Atkinson 1983). During the 1980s, an era of regressive taxation and recession, there is some evidence to suggest that the poor in both countries have got poorer (Moon and Sawhill 1984; Walker and Walker, 1987; Winnick 1989).

As far as the second type of data is concerned, in Britain occupational class income data go back over a century (Routh 1987), but in America reliable statistics are available for the post-war period only (Levy 1987). Both sets of official statistics show a consistent relationship between class and income, and the necessity of disaggregating the earnings of men and women. Moreover, in the USA official statistics and sociological research have revealed a clear racial dimension to income inequality (Levy 1987; Wright 1979). In sum, the British and American data show that throughout the periods for which data are available:

1 The 'higher' the occupational class the higher the average pay/mean earnings and vice versa (Routh 1987: 79; Levy 1987: 128–9).
2 The average pay/median income is higher for employed men than for employed women at all levels of the occupational class structure (Routh 1987: 79; Levy 1987: 142).
3 In the USA white men have a higher median income than black men and the gap is widening, and white women have a higher median income than black women and the gap is narrowing (Levy 1987: 137 and 142).

A partial exception to the traditional ways of presenting data on class and inequality is the work of Wright, who has analysed the

Table 6.1 Mean annual individual incomes by class in the USA

Class location	Income ($)
1 Bourgeoisie	52,621
2 Small employers	24,828
3 Petty bourgeoisie	14,496
4 Expert manager	28,665
5 Expert supervisors	23,057
6 Expert non-manager	15,251
7 Semi-credentialled manager	20,701
8 Semi-credentialled supervisors	18,023
9 Semi-credentialled workers	16,034
10 Uncredentialled manager	12,276
11 Uncredentialled supervisors	13,045
12 Proletarians	11,161

Source: Adapted from Wright 1985: 235

relationship between his neo-Marxist classes and income (see Chapter 2). On the basis of both his first and his later models of the class structure, Wright has confirmed that income is clearly structured by class (1979 and 1985). In the example of the class distribution of income presented in Table 6.1, the class scheme is Wright's neo-Marxist class map II, the unit of analysis is the individual, the degree of coverage is the economically active, and the income data is based on a respondent's total personal income from all sources before taxation for the previous year.

Table 6.1 shows that in contemporary America, income is clearly polarized between the large owners of capital, the bourgeoisie, and the workers at the base of the class structure and that 'incomes vary monotonically along the dimensions of exploitation taken separately and together' (Wright 1985: 237). In this survey of class and income inequality, the characteristic exclusion of the economically inactive, e.g. the unemployed, students, housewives and pensioners, understates the magnitude of the gap between the wealthy capitalist class and the poorest members of society. The salience of this point is underlined by the alleged recent expansion of the underclass in Britain and in America in the context of reduced welfare state spending (Edgell and Duke 1991; Kreiger 1986).

However it is measured, all the available historical and comparative data on class and economic inequality show that class is the major influence on the distribution of wealth and income in modern societies. This pattern is so well established that many sociologists, especially in America, use income as a substitute measure for the identification of class, either on its own or in combination with other proxy variables (Gilbert and Kahl 1987). However, the use of income as a single proxy variable for indicating class is problematic, especially in research samples that include both men and women, given the persistence of gender differences in income within classes.

In addition to showing that class can affect your income and wealth, these data suggest that the ownership of capital, the key dimension of class inequality in the sense that it is the source of the greatest economic inequality in society, is less unequal than in the past but still very marked in Britain and America, and possibly increasing. In other words, the continued concentration of wealth is an important part of the distinctiveness of the capitalist class, a class that is often hidden in much sociological research. Class inequality of income has remained more stable over time, and there are occupational, gender and racial variations within the overall historical pattern. In the context of a higher standard of living for all over time, plus the creation of state welfare systems, these trends in class inequality broadly support Marx's theoretical expectations regarding the class nature of the persistence of economic inequality in general and that of an underclass in particular. However, it remains to be seen if the recent evidence of increased economic polarization in Britain and America, at a time of recession and reduced welfare spending, is a temporary phenomenon or the start of a new era.

THE DEMOCRATIC CLASS STRUGGLE

The class basis of politics was fully appreciated by Marx and Weber, who both noted that modern political parties represent the economic interests of different classes. For Marx, his theory of revolutionary change was based on the assumption that the material interests of the working class are best served by supporting a socialist party. But Weber qualified his class analysis of parties by commenting that they 'need be neither purely "class" nor purely "status" parties' (1961: 194).

In post-war Britain and America it was widely thought that support for the major political parties followed class lines in that the 'middle' classes tended to vote for a right-wing party and the 'lower' classes for a left-wing party (Lipset 1963). The logic behind these established tendencies was that the main political parties, from right to left as it were, Conservative and Labour in Britain, Republican and Democratic in America, primarily represent the economic interests of capital and labour respectively in the context of appearing to appeal to the widest possible range of electors. This is readily apparent from their policies which, whilst claiming to offer the best programme for the country as a whole, tend to favour either capital, and therefore greater inequality (e.g. tax reliefs for businesses and the better-off), or labour, and therefore greater equality (e.g. state benefits for workers and the less well-off). This is reflected in the tendency for trade unions to contribute financially to left-wing parties, and for business organizations to right-wing parties, as well as by the working class/left and middle class/right voting patterns.

This conventional wisdom regarding the class basis of political parties in terms of both electoral and financial support was well summed up by the American sociologist Lipset:

In every modern democracy conflict among different groups is expressed through political parties which basically represent a 'democratic translation of the class struggle.' Even though many parties renounce the principle of class conflict or loyalty, an analysis of their appeals and their support suggests that they do represent the interests of different classes. On a world scale, the principal generalization which can be made is that parties are primarily based on either the lower classes or the middle and upper classes. This generalization even holds true for the American parties, which have traditionally been considered an exception to the class-cleavage pattern of Europe.

(1963: 220)

The clear relationship between class and voting behaviour in Britain and America was evident in all the social survey and election studies data throughout the immediate post-war era. For example, Lipset (1963) quoted 1950s data to show that the majority of the 'middle' classes voted for the Conservative party in Britain and for the Republican party in America whereas the majority of the 'working' classes voted for the Labour party and the Democratic party. The link between class and political behaviour is, however, less marked in America compared to Britain and other European nations (Alford 1963), and according to Gilbert and Kahl (1987) there are two main reasons for this. First, the American Democratic party is more 'liberal' than 'socialist' and therefore tends to be less partisan of the working class. Second, race and ethnicity tend to cut across class cleavages thereby weakening the association between class and party. The comparatively limited class bias of American politics is part of the debate about American exceptionalism (see Chapter 4 and Piven 1991).

Explanations of why some people vote against their 'natural' class interests also involves class theory. Typically, it is argued that class marginality characterizes working-class rightists, for example, farm labourers (Lipset 1963), and also middle-class leftists, for example, upwardly mobile managers (Abramson 1972). In other words, atypical members of the working class are more likely to vote for a right-wing party, and atypical members of the middle class are more likely to vote for a left-wing party.

(For a recent discussion of this issue with reference to British data see Heath and Evans 1988.)

During the 1970s and 1980s, some electoral analysts in Britain (e.g. Butler and Stokes 1974; Sarlvik and Crewe 1983) and America (e.g. Flanigan and Zingale 1975; Ladd and Hadley 1978), challenged the class-vote orthodoxy by claiming that the historical relationship between class and party support was in decline. This decline was attributed to changes in the class structure and class relationships, notably increased affluence, reduced conflict and general class fragmentation, but rarely explained in detail.

One of the fullest accounts of the theory of class dealignment has been provided by Dalton (1988) in his review of post-war class voting patterns in selected western democracies, including Britain and America. He operationalized class on an essentially occupational basis (i.e. manual working class and a non-manual middle class which included the old and the new middle classes). He measured class voting using the Alford index, which is a relative measure of class alignment that is calculated by subtracting the left's percentage share of the vote among non-manual workers from its share among manual workers (Alford 1963). In other words, conventionally it is left voting that is used as the basis for calculating this index of class voting, but it is just as simple, though less usual, to use right voting. Dalton showed a secular decline in class voting over time and claimed that this 'reflects a general trend of weakening socio-economic cleavages' (1988: 158).

Dalton advanced three main reasons for the decline in class voting: first, that changes in the class structure, such as the proletarianization of certain white-collar workers and the embourgeoisement of certain blue-collar workers, has lessened class differences and has led to the 'convergence of class voting patterns' (Dalton 1988: 158). Second and relatedly, he argued that high rates of social mobility tend 'to blur traditional class and partisan alignments' (1988: 159). Third, he claimed that parties had become ideologically less classist since 1945 in an attempt to broaden 'their electoral appeals . . . to attract centrist voters' (1988: 159). Thus, for Dalton, 'the decline in class voting patterns represents both a weakening of the voters' class identities and a narrowing of party positions on class-based issues' (1988: 159). Dalton's theory of class dealignment is comparable to less detailed accounts, for example, Butler and Stokes (1974).

The thesis that class voting has declined in western democracies has been evaluated more critically in Britain, notably by Heath and his research associates (Heath *et al.* 1985; Heath *et al.* 1991), than in America, where class dealignment seems to be taken for granted (Ladd 1989).

On the basis of the distinction between absolute and relative rates of class voting, in other words between 'the overall proportion of voters who support the party of their class' and 'the relative strength of a particular party in different social classes' (Heath *et al.* 1991: 64), Heath and his associates show that absolute class voting has declined but that relative class voting has changed very little. They conclude that in Britain, 'there may have been a very modest amount of class secularization (perhaps due to processes like social mobility) but it has only minimal relevance to explaining political change' (Heath *et al.* 1991: 78).

This critique of class dealignment has in turn been the subject of extensive critical commentary. For example, it has been noted that their neo-Weberian class scheme involves a major reduction in the size of the working class (Crewe 1986; Dunleavy 1987), and that there are important production sector related political divisions within the 'service class' (Savage *et al.* 1992: 190). Also, their measure of relative class voting has been criticized by Crewe who has argued that 'in elections, unlike election books, it is absolute numbers, not relative probabilities, that count' (1986: 638), and Dunleavy (1987) who has claimed that it is distortingly over-sensitive to small changes in class voting.

A further contentious aspect of the theory of class dealignment concerns the claim that the working class has become less solidaristic politically. However, few if any systematic data are presented in support of this assertion (Goldthorpe 1987; Heath *et al.* 1985; Heath et al. 1991). Moreover, the thesis that class and party differences have lessened is difficult to maintain in the light of the persistence of class inequalities and class consciousness (Marshall *et al.* 1988; Vanneman and Cannon 1987), and the ideological polarization of party politics under the Thatcher and Reagan administrations during the 1980s (Edgell and Duke 1991; Krieger 1986). Thus, for the theory of class dealignment to be credible, it would need to be shown that class interests, and the ideologies that express them, have a declining influence on voters and parties.

It is noticeable that neither the proponents nor the opponents of class dealignment are saying that class is no longer relevant to political attitudes and behaviour; it is more a matter of the extent of the association between class and vote over time, including non-voting (cf. Piven 1991). For example, Dalton (1988) has acknowledged that class is still an influence on voting behaviour, but claims that it has declined during the post-war era. By the some token, Heath *et al.* have conceded that 'a modest process of class secularization probably did occur' (1991: 78). There have always been cross-class voters, with leftist parties attracting 'middle' class support and rightist parties attracting 'working' class support. However, as Lipset, echoing Veblen (1970), has noted, 'conservative parties have the advantage of being identified with the more prestigeful classes in the population, an appeal which helps to overcome the left's appeal to the economic interests of the lower classes' (1963: 230).

From the beginning of the debate therefore, the concept of cross-class voting has been predicated on the assumption that parties represent class interests, yet the proponents of class dealignment typically base their analysis on a class scheme that makes no reference to the economic interests of different classes (e.g. Butler and Stokes 1974), and the opponents of class dealignment base their anlaysis on a class scheme that makes reference to class interests but excludes the large-scale owners of capital (e.g. Heath *et al.* 1985). Thus, there is very little direct evidence on Marx's class interests theory of politics 'since no empirical studies use class in his sense' (Robinson and Kelley 1979). One of the possible reasons for this is the problem of identifying empirically large-scale owners in the era of corporate or organizational capitalism where the major 'employer' is more likely to be a pension fund than a person (Erikson and Goldthorpe 1992). Consequently, when an attempt is made to distinguish major from minor owners, the capitalist class tends to contain a predominance of medium-size employers, although there is no denying their political distinctiveness (Edgell and Duke 1991).

SUMMARY AND CONCLUSIONS

Notwithstanding the measurement controversies that surround the debates about class inequality and class politics, this chapter has shown that the concept of class remains central to the analysis of both debates in America and Britain. Thus the pivotal role assigned to class in the classic perspectives of Marx and Weber is still relevant to the analysis of modern societies. This is not to suggest that class is the only factor that structures economic and political life, but it is arguably the most fundamental.

In the case of the distribution of economic rewards, the major inequalities relate to the ownership of private property for exchange, the persistence of which is indicative of the continued importance of inheritance. Although education is relevant to income inequalities, the acquisition of credentials is itself influenced by class. Non-class factors, notably gender and race/ethnicity, are also relevant to the patterning of economic inequality, but are of secondary rather than primary importance. There is some evidence of a slight decline in economic inequality in America and Britain during the post-war era. However, the continued concentration of wealth at the top of the class structure, and of poverty at the bottom, broadly conforms to Marx's theoretical expectations.

The post-war orthodoxy that there was a clear relationship between class and vote was challenged in Britain and America during the 1970s and 1980s by class dealignment theorists. The ensuing debate centred around how best to measure class voting trends and involved a variety of approaches to the issue of class operationalization. The net result was a lively and at times a highly technical debate, the resolution of which depends in large part on the measure of class voting selected. Thus, absolute class voting may well have declined, whereas relative class voting seems to have changed very little.

Considered together, the two themes of this chapter suggest that class, however measured, is still relevant to an understanding of social life in contemporary industrial capitalist societies such as Britain and America. More specifically, the pattering of economic inequality and politics remains class related, although the degree of influence continues to be the subject of considerable debate. Thus, the 'withering away' of class, as it is sometimes referred to (cf. Westergaard and Resler 1975: 17), is a sociological fantasy, and the subject of the next and final chapter.

7

Classlessness and the end of class

INTRODUCTION

The main theme throughout this study of class has been on the continued importance of the theoretical traditions founded by Marx and Weber. Notwithstanding their differing emphases, in the words of Weber, they both argued that the ownership of property for exchange and propertylessness are 'the basic categories of all class situations' (1961: 182). However, they both differentiated several other classes in recognition of the dynamic nature of capitalist societies, although Weber's account of class was the more pluralistic. The sociological significance of classes, thus defined, is that class relationships are the key to the analysis of the social structure in general, and economic and political life in particular. It is in this sense that it may be asserted that industrial capitalist nations, such as Britain and America, are still class societies.

With respect to the future of class societies and classlessness, the seminal contributions of Marx and Weber provide our point of departure yet once more. For Marx, the end of capitalism, and therefore of class, was to be achieved via the revolutionary overthrow of the capitalist class by the working class, the abolition of private property, and the establishment of a classless society based on equality of condition. However, after a successful revolution, there would be a transitional period in which the new ruling class, the proletariat, would dismantle capitalism. This may be called the one-class society stage of classlessness. Only when the old conditions of production that gave rise to class conflict have been been swept away, and with them all class distinctions, will it be possible to inaugurate a classless society 'in which the free development of each is the condition for the free development of all' (Marx and Engels 1848: 90). Thus, in Marx's theory of social change, multi-class conflict societies of the present are compared unfavourably with one-class classlessness and totally classless societies of the future.

In marked contrast, for Weber there was no escape from the 'iron cage' of 'victorious capitalism' (1976: 181). He argued that: 'More and more the material fate of the masses depends upon the steady and correct functioning of the increasingly bureaucratic organizations of private capitalism. The idea of eliminating these organizations becomes more and more utopian' (Weber 1961: 229). For Weber, bureaucratic domination was inescapable due to the technical superiority of this type of organization, and socialism would exacerbate rather than ameliorate the problem. Whereas, thanks to their superior business expertise: 'The capitalistic entrepreneur is, in our society, the only type who has been able to maintain at least relative immunity from subjection to the control of rational bureaucratic knowledge' (1964: 339). In addition, Weber noted that bureaucratization involves 'equality of treatment' which 'greatly favours the levelling of social classes . . . for it tends to eliminate class privileges' (1964: 340), although the levelling process is limited to the governed in contradistinction to the 'ruling and bureaucratically articulated group' (1961: 226). Moreover, Weber was concerned with the virtually indestructible nature of bureaucratic power and the possibility of social closure among positively privileged classes based on the possession of property or credentials. Thus, although Weber expressed reservations about the anti-democratic nature of bureaucratization, he discussed classlessness in terms of equality of opportunity following the decline of differentiation and privilege which he associated with the increasing pervasiveness of bureaucratic structures in all spheres of society.

Thus, in the final analysis, there is a clear divergence between

Marx and Weber on the future of class societies, with regard to the capitalist as villain or hero and the domination of capital or bureaucratic domination. In sum, Marx was concerned with the subordination of the proletariat to the rule of capital and thought that the abolition of the property basis of class was the first essential step in the achievement of a truly classless society. Weber, on the other hand, argued that the elimination of the capitalist class would lead to an increase in subordination to the bureaucratically empowered. Hence, he favoured the rationality of a bureaucratically organized capitalist system with its equality of opportunity, and increased but limited social levelling.

CONTEMPORARY CONCEPTIONS OF CLASSLESSNESS

Contemporary views on the idea of classlessness can all be traced to a greater or lesser extent to the Marxian and Weberian contributions to the sociology of class. There are three main conceptions of classlessness; total classlessness, one-class classlessness, and multi-class classlessness.

Total classlessness is a neo-Marxist conception that involves the abolition of private property – the basis of capitalist power over the working class and the main source of economic inequality. To ensure success, it would also be necessary to abolish inheritance, implement a progressive taxation system, provide free education and health for all, and prevent any one social group from monopolizing political power and exercising it in their own interests.

This is an extreme version of classlessness and as such it is very problematic. First, it is highly ambitious in that it assumes the complete transformation of a class society and all that that implies in terms of overcoming internal and external opposition. Second, this type of classlessness contradicts the alleged universal functional necessity for stratification (Davis and Moore 1945). According to this theory, social stratification solves the problem faced by all societies of motivating people to fill the functionally important positions and perform the roles associated with them. Third, a related line of argument is that total classlessness is impossible in any society characterized by a highly differentiated occupational division of labour and a solidary kinship system (Parsons 1952). Fourth and finally, this conception of classlessness implies social harmony, yet conflict performs valuable functions in all societies (Coser 1956). For example, conflict can not only change relationships, it can also transform whole societies. Thus, the case against total classlessness is that it is unrealistic. Whatever the merits and demerits of functionalism (for a critique of the functionalist theory of stratification see Tumin 1953), at the very least there are numerous social and political obstacles which threaten the achievement of total classlessness.

One-class classlessness can take two forms; a 'working-class' society and a 'middle-class' society. An example of the former variant is the Soviet or communist type of society in the transitional stage, characterized by a form of government that is often referred to as the 'dictatorship of the proletariat'. (It is important to note that this term did not have the same pejorative meaning for Marx that it does for us today; for a brief discussion of this point see McLellan 1971.) From a variety of neo-Marxist and non-Marxist perspectives (see Parkin 1971), it has been argued that in such a society there are no classes because there is no private property and there is no class conflict because everybody shares the same relationship to the means of production. Social and economic differentiation prevails, but does not lead to the formation of classes due to a high rate of social mobility. The main but temporary social division is between the omnipresent Communist Party bureaucracy and the non-Party citizenry. However, having been inspired by the Marxian theory of revolutionary class change, this type of one-class classlessness arguably conformed to the tendency noted by Weber (1961 and 1964), for a stratum to develop into a hierocracy that monopolizes state power and enjoys the associated economic advantages. Thus, the failure of Soviet-type societies to progress beyond the first stage, in which the means of administration are concentrated in the hands of a few, seems to have resulted in the shattering of the 'practically unshatterable' (Weber 1961: 228).

An example of the 'middle-class' variant of one-class classlessness is the argument that everybody is middle class in societies like contemporary Britain and America (Mayer 1956, 1959 and 1963; Zweig 1961). This conception of classlessness is part of the debate about embourgeoisement (discussed briefly in Chapter 4), and as such suffers from all the well documented limitations of this thesis (Goldthorpe *et al.* 1969). It was claimed that increasing prosperity and changes in the occupational structure were leading to a reduction in income differentials and an equalization of consumption patterns, and that as a consequence of these economic trends, class conflict and class differences were declining.

There was also a political dimension to this thesis, namely that affluence encouraged conservatism and discouraged radicalism. Thus, 'middle-classness' was evident everywhere, at work, home, play and in politics. This thesis always seemed to be more popular among social commentators than sociologists (see the sources cited by Goldthorpe *et al.* 1969), and once it had been subjected to systematic and critical appraisal, it was shown to be lacking in credibility. Economic cycles of boom and slump still occur, economic insecurity and inequality have not diminished, consumption standards have certainly increased but for all classes not just the working class, at best class conflict has been institutionalized, but it has not disappeared, and so-called affluent workers continued to support leftist parties. Thus, the notion of middle-class classlessness is a myth; it is based on false assumptions, evidence and theory.

Considered together, working class classlessness and middle-class classlessness are post-capitalist accounts of societal development in that they both assume that the classic property-based owner–worker dichotomy has been transcended. Thus, the first variant is predicated on the disappearance of the intermediate class, the second variant is predicated on the disappearance of the working class, and both deny the existence of dominant classes. Neither the abolition of private property and the alleged proletarianization of communist-type societies, nor the depersonalization of private property and the alleged embourgeoisement of capitalist type societies, have reduced the concentration of economic power in either of these types of society.

Multi-class classlessness refers to societies where civic equality co-exists with the progressive fragmentation of the class structure and class consciousness. This highly pluralistic conception of classlesness has its origins in Weber's analysis of classes in modern (i.e. bureaucratic and democratic) capitalism and reaches its zenith in the functionalist model of social stratification. Thus, multi-class classlessness involves the equal opportunity to be unequal and has been called non-egalitarian classlessness (Ossowski 1963). According to Ossowski (1963: 107) this conception of classlessness has the following features:

1 'The social and economic status of individuals is not determined by descent; the road to the highest positions is open to all, even though they may not have an equal start.'
2 'The social-status scale is not broken by any distinct bar-

riers which could transform the continuum-like status order
into a gradation of different strata.'
3 'In accordance with the last condition no definite privileges
are attached to the various segments of that scale, nor do
any permanent conflicts of interest exist between higher
and lower levels of social status.'
4 'There is no separation or restriction in social contacts
between strata.'

This conceptualization of classlessness is congruent with the basic
tenet of the American Creed, namely civic equality (Ossowski
1963), and with the defining values of American society, notably
equality of opportunity and individual success (Williams 1970).
It is therefore a description of the American Dream in that it
emphasizes the possibility that anyone can achieve upward social
mobility. The political importance of this type of classlessness is
that it attributes inequalities to variations in individual ability,
thereby legitimizing social differentiation. This view is not unique
to America, but is a part of the ideology of late capitalism
(Abercrombie et al. 1980). In Britain, classlessness of this kind
was advocated by John Major during his campaign for the leadership of the Conservative Party and the country: 'I think we need
a classless society, and I think we need to have what I refer to
as social mobility. And what I mean by social mobility is the
capacity of everybody to have the help necessary to achieve the
maximum for their ability (*Guardian* 28 November 1990).

Non-egalitarian classlessness has long been recognized, even
in America, as a contradictory social construction since if everybody is equal, there can be no superior or inferior positions to
move into (Warner 1960). Moreover, in a hierarchical society,
not everyone can be successful, otherwise the chiefs would out-
number the Indians. Studies that focus on the social consequences
of the failure to achieve the American Dream, such as the stress
on consumer satisfaction (Chinoy 1955), status panic (Mills 1956),
deviance (Merton 1968), and guilt and social humiliation (Sennett
and Cobb 1977), are indicative of its inherent contradictions.
Over and above the hidden and not so 'hidden injuries of class'
(Sennett and Cobb 1977), the fundamental objection to multi-
class classlessness is that the persistence of marked economic
inequalities and the constancy of relative mobility rates confirm
the continued importance of the generational transmission of
economic and cultural capital. For this type of classlessness to

become more than just a dream for the majority of the subordinate classes, class inheritance would have to be severely curtailed. In other words, political intervention would be required to remove the inequalities of condition that impede equality of opportunity and the achievement of a truly open society (Goldthorpe 1987).

SUMMARY AND CONCLUSIONS

The traditions of class analysis founded by Marx and Weber extend from a consideration of the origins and nature of class in industrial capitalist societies, to a concern with the idea of classlessness and the future of class societies. The three main conceptualizations of classlessness outlined, namely total classlessness, one-class classlessness and multi-class classlessness, can all be related to the works of Marx and Weber to a greater or lesser extent. Arguably, the least unrealistic of all the conceptualizations of classlessness considered is the multi-class version in the important sense that there are no formal barriers to upward mobility. The class system of modern capitalism is an impersonal and relatively open one, and provides the context in which the idea of classlessness may exert a powerful influence. However, as indicated by Marx and Weber, there are many inherently contradictory or conflicting elements that prevent the achievement of non-egalitarian classlessness. For example, Marx emphasized, and Weber mentioned, the opposition of class interests between the owners of property and the sellers of labour power in the market. In addition, Weber drew attention to the tendency for positively privileged classes to monopolize opportunities and the difficulty of controlling bureaucratic power. Thus the main obstacle to the establishment of a multi-class or non-egalitarian classless democratic society is the persistence of class inequalities, whether they are based on the ownership of property and/or the possession of credentials, in the context of a highly bureaucratized capitalist society. Hence, what needs to be explained is not the presumed demise of class, but the tenacity of class-based patterns of inequality and politics, and much else besides. In the meantime, class rules and classlessness remains a dream rather than a reality.

References

Abbott, P. (1990) 'A re-examination of "Three theses re-examined" ', in G. Payne and P. Abbott (eds) *The Social Mobility of Women: Beyond Male Mobility Models*, London: Falmer Press.

Abbott, P. and Sapsford, R. (1987) *Women and Social Class*, London: Tavistock.

Abbott, P. and Wallace, C. (1990) *An Introduction to Sociology: Feminist Perspectives*, London: Routledge.

Abercrombie, N. et al. (1980) *The Dominant Ideology Thesis*, London: Allen & Unwin.

Abercrombie, N. and Urry, J. (1983) *Capital, Labour and the Middle Classes*, London: Allen & Unwin.

Abramson, P. (1972) 'Intergenerational social mobility and partisan choice', *American Political Science Review*, 66: 1291–94.

Acker, J. (1973) 'Women and social stratification', *American Journal of Sociology*, 78: 936–45.

Ahrne, G. (1990) 'Class and society: a critique of John Goldthorpe's model of social classes' in J. Clark et al. (eds) *John H. Goldthorpe: Consensus and Controversy*, London: Falmer Press.

Alford, R. (1963) *Party and Society*, Chicago: Rand McNally.

Allen, P. (ed.) (1963) *Pitirim A. Sorokin in Review*, Durham: Duke University Press.

Arber, S. et al. (1986) 'The limitations of existing social class classifications of women', in A. Jacoby (ed.) *The Measurement of Social Class*, London: Social Research Association.

Aron, R. (1972) *Progress and Disillusion*, London: Pelican.

Aronowitz, S. (1974) *The Shaping of American Working Class Consciousness*, New York: McGraw-Hill.

Atkinson, A. (1974) 'Poverty and income inequality in Britain', in D. Wedderburn (ed.) *Poverty, Inequality and Class Structure*, Cambridge: Cambridge University Press.

—— (1980) *Wealth, Income and Inequality*, Oxford: Oxford University Press (second edition).

—— (1983) *The Economics of Inequality*, Oxford: Clarendon Press (second edition).

Attewell, P. (1989) 'The clerk deskilled: a study in false nostalgia', *Journal of Historical Sociology*, 2: 357–88.

Auletta, K. (1982) *The Underclass*, New York: Random House.

Bagguley, P. and Mann, K. (1992) 'Idle thieving bastards? Scholarly representations of the "underclass" ', *Work, Employment and Society*, 6: 113–26.

Baran, P. and Sweezy, P. (1968) *Monopoly Capital*, London: Pelican.

Bechhofer, F. et al. (1974) 'The petits bourgeois in the class structure' in F. Parkin (ed.) *The Social Analysis of Class Structure*, London: Tavistock.

Bechhofer, F. and Elliot, B. (1978) 'The politics of survival' in J. Garrard et al. (eds) *The Middle Class in Politics*, Farnborough: Saxon House.

—— (1981) *The Petite Bourgeoisie*, London: Macmillan.

Bendix, R. (1960) *Max Weber: an Intellectual Portrait*, London: Heinemann.

Berle, A. A. and Means, G. C. (1968) *The Modern Corporation and Private Property*, New York: Harcourt, Brace & World Inc. (revised edition, first published in 1932).

Berlin, I. (1963), *Karl Marx*, London: Oxford University Press.

Blackburn, R. (1965) 'The new capitalism' in P. Anderson and R. Blackburn (eds) *Towards Socialism*, London: Fontana.

Blackburn, R. and Mann, M. (1979) *The Working Class in the Labour Market*, London: Macmillan.

Bland, R. (1979) 'Measuring "social class" ', *Sociology*, 13: 283–91.

Blau, P. M. and Duncan, O. R. (1967) *The American Occupational Structure*, New York: Wiley.

Bogenhold, D. and Staber, U. (1991) 'The decline and rise of self-employment', *Work, Employment and Society* 5: 223–39.

Boissevain, J. (1984) 'Small entrepreneurs in contemporary Europe' in R. Ward and R. Jenkins (eds) *Ethnic Communities in Business*, Cambridge: Cambridge University Press.

Boston, G. (1980) 'Classification of occupations', *Population Trends*, 20: 9–11.

Bottomore, T. (1989) 'The capitalist class' in T. Bottomore and R. Brym (eds) *The Capitalist Class: an International Study*, London: Harvester-Wheatsheaf.

—— (1991) *Classes in Modern Society*, London: HarperCollins (revised edition, first published in 1965).

Bottomore, T. et al. (eds) (1991) *A Dictionary of Marxist Thought*, Oxford: Blackwell (second edition).

Bourdieu, P. (1971) 'Cultural reproduction and social reproduction', *Social Science Information*, 20: 45–99.

—— (1984) *Distinction: a Social Critique of the Judgement of Taste*, London: Routledge and Kegan Paul.

Braverman, H. (1974) *Labour and Monopoly Capital: the Degradation of Work in the Twentieth Century*, New York: Monthly Review Press.

Brewer, R. (1986) 'A note on the changing status of the Registrar General's classification of occupations', *British Journal of Sociology*, 37: 131–40.

Britten, N. and Heath, A. (1983) 'Women, men and social class', in E. Gamarnikow et al. (eds) *Gender, Class and Work*, London: Heinemann.

Brown, C. (1984) *Black and White Britain*, London: Heinemann.

Brown, R. (1990) 'A flexible future in Europe? Changing patterns of employment in the United Kingdom', *British Journal of Sociology*, 41: 301–327.

Burnham, J. (1945) *The Managerial Revolution*, London: Pelican (first published in 1941).

Burrows, R. (ed.) (1991) *Deciphering the Enterprise Culture: Entrepreneurship, Petty Capitalism and the Restructuring of Britain*, London: Routledge.

Burrows, R. and Curran, J. (1989) 'Sociological research on

the service sector small businesses', *Work, Employment and Society*, 3: 527–39.

Butler, D. and Stokes, D. (1974) *Political Change in Britain*, London: Macmillan.

Carchedi, G. (1977) *On the Economic Identification of Social Classes*, London: Routledge and Kegan Paul.

—— (1989) 'Classes and class analysis', in E.O. Wright (ed.) *The Debate on Classes*, London: Verso.

Carter, R. (1985) *Capitalism, Class Conflict and the New Middle Class*, London: Routledge and Kegan Paul.

Carter, R. (1986) 'Review of classes', *Sociological Review*, 34: 686–8.

Child, J. (1969) *The Business Enterprise in Modern Industrial Society*, London: Macmillan.

Chinoy, E. (1955) *Automobile Workers and the American Dream*, Boston: Beacon.

Clegg, S. et al. (1986) *Class, Politics and the Economy*, London: Routledge.

Cohen, J. and Rogers, J. (1988) 'Reaganism after Reagan' in R. Miliband (ed.) *The Socialist Register*, London: Merlin.

Collins, R. (1979) *The Credential Society*, London: Academic Press.

Conk, M. A. (1978) 'Occupational classification in the United States census: 1870–1940', *Journal of Interdisciplinary History*, 9: 111–30.

Cornforth, C. et al. (1988) *Developing Successful Worker Co-operatives*, London: Sage.

Coser, L. (1956) *The Functions of Social Conflict*, Glencoe: Free Press.

—— (1977) *Masters of Sociological Thought: Ideas in Historical and Social Context*, New York: Harcourt Brace Jovanovich (second edition).

Coxon, A. et al. (1986) *Images of Social Stratification*, London: Sage.

Crewe, I. (1986) 'On the death and resurrection of class voting: some comments on "*How Britain Votes*" ', *Political Studies*, 34: 620–38.

Crompton, R. (1990) 'Goldthorpe and Marxist theories of historical development' in J. Clark et al. (eds) *John H. Goldthorpe: Consensus and Controversy*, London: Falmer Press.

Crompton, R. and Gubbay, J. (1977) *Economy and Class Structure*, London: Macmillan.

Crompton, R. and Jones, G. (1984) *White Collar Proletariat*, London: Macmillan.

Crompton, R. and Mann, M. (1986) *Gender and Stratification*, Cambridge: Cambridge University Press.

Crompton, R. and Reid, S. (1983) 'The deskilling of clerical work' in S. Wood (ed.) *The Degradation of Work*, London: Hutchinson.

Crossland, C. (1964) *The Future of Socialism*, London: Cape (first published in 1956).

Crowder, N. (1974) 'A critique of Duncan's stratification research', *Sociology*, 8: 19–45.

Curran, J. and Burrows, R. (1986) 'The sociology of petite capitalism', *Sociology*, 20: 265–79.

Curran, J. et al. (eds) (1986) *The Survival of the Small Firm I: the Economics and Survival of Entrepreneurship*, Aldershot: Gower.

Cutler, A. (1978) 'The romance of labour', *Economy and Society*, 7: 74–9.

Dahrendorf, R. (1959) *Class and Class Conflict in an Industrial Society*, London: Routledge and Kegan Paul.

—— (1964) 'Recent changes in the class structure of European societies', *Daedalus*, 93: 225–70.

Dale, A. et al. (1985) 'Integrating women into class theory', *Sociology*, 19: 384–408.

Dalton, R. (1988) *Citizen Politics in Western Democracies*, Chatham, NJ: Chatham House.

Davies, C. (1980) 'Making sense of the census in Britain and the USA', *Sociological Review*, 28: 581–609.

Davis, K. and Moore, W. (1945) 'Some principles of stratification', *American Sociological Review*, 10: 242–9.

Delphy, C. (1981) 'Women in stratification studies' in H. Roberts (ed.) *Doing Feminist Research*, London: Routledge and Kegan Paul.

De Vroey, M. (1975) 'The corporation and the labor process: the separation of ownership and control in large corporations', *Review of Radical Political Economics*, 7: 1–10.

Devine, F. (1992) *Affluent Workers Revisited*, Edinburgh: Edinburgh University Press.

Dex, S. (1985) *The Sexual Division of Work*, Brighton: Wheatsheaf.

—— (1987) *Women's Occupational Mobility*, London: Macmillan.

—— (1990) 'Goldthorpe on class and gender: the case against' in J. Clark et al. (eds) *John H. Goldthorpe: Consensus and Controversy*, London: Falmer Press.

Domhoff, G. (1967) *Who Rules America?*, New Jersey: Prentice Hall.

Drudy, S. (1991) 'The classification of social class in sociological research', *British Journal of Sociology*, 42: 21–41.

Duke, V. and Edgell, S. (1987) 'The operationalization of class in British sociology', *British Journal of Sociology* 38: 445–63.

Dunleavy, P. (1980) *Urban Political Analysis*, London: Macmillan.

Dunleavy, P. (1987) 'Class dealignment in Britain revisited', *West European Politics*, 10: 400–19.

Dunleavy, P. and Husbands, C. (1985) *British Democracy at the Crossroads*, London: Allen & Unwin.

Edgell, S. (1980) *Middle Class Couples*, London: Allen and Unwin.

—— (1987) 'Veblen: social theorist and social critic', *Salford Papers in Sociology* no. 3, Salford: University of Salford.

—— (1989) Book review of *Status* by B.S. Turner, *Sociology*, 23: 647–8.

—— (1992) 'Veblen and post-Veblen studies of conspicuous consumption: social stratification and fashion', *Revue Internationale de Sociologie*, Nouvelle Serie – N3: 205–27.

Edgell, S. and Duke, V. (1983) 'Gender and social policy: the impact of the public expenditure cuts and reactions to them', *Journal of Social Policy*, 12: 357–78.

—— (1986) 'Radicalism, radicalization and recession', *British Journal of Sociology*, 37: 479–512.

—— (1991) *A Measure of Thatcherism: a Sociology of Britain* London: HarperCollins.

Edgell, S. and Hart, G. (1988) 'Informal work: a case study of moonlighting firemen', *Salford Papers in Sociology* no. 6 Salford: University of Salford.

Edgell, S. and Tilman, R. (1991) 'John Rae and Thorstein Veblen on conspicuous consumption', *History of Political Economy* 23: 167–180.

Edgell, S. and Townshend, J. (1992) 'John Hobson, Thorstein Veblen and the phenomenon of imperialism: finance capital patriotism and war', *American Journal of Economics and Sociology*, 51: 401–20.

Erikson, R. (1984) 'Social class of men, women and families', *Sociology*, 18: 500–14.

Erikson, R. and Goldthorpe, J.H. (1985) 'Are American rates of social mobility exceptionally high? New evidence on an old issue', *European Sociological Review*, 1: 1–22.

—— (1992) *The Constant Flux: a Study of Class Mobility in Industrial Societies*, Oxford: Clarendon Press.

Erikson, R., Goldthorpe, J.H., and Portocarero, L. (1979) 'Intergenerational class mobility in three western European societies: England, France and Sweden', *British Journal of Sociology*, 30: 415–41.

—— (1982) 'Social fluidity in industrial nations: England, France and Sweden', *British Journal of Sociology*, 33: 1–34.

—— (1983) 'International social mobility and the convergence thesis', *British Journal of Sociology*, 34: 303–43.

Evans, G. (1992) 'Is Britain a class-divided society?', *Sociology*, 26: 233–58.

Featherman, D. (1981) 'Social stratification and mobility: two decades of cumulative social science', *American Behavioral Scientist*, 24: 364–85.

Featherman, D. and Hauser, R. (1978) *Opportunity and Change*, New York: Academic Press.

Fevre, R. (1991) 'Emerging "alternatives" to full-time and permanent employment' in P. Brown and R. Scase (eds) *Poor Work: Disadvantage and the Division of Labour*, Milton Keynes: Open University.

Field, F. (1989) *Losing Out: the Emergence of Britain's Underclass*, Oxford: Blackwell.

Finch, J. (1983) *Married to the Job*, London: Allen and Unwin.

Flanigan, W. and Zingale, N. (1975) *Political Behaviour of the American Electorate*, Boston: Allyn and Bacon (third edition).

Ford, J. (1989) 'Casual work and owner occupation', *Work, Employment and Society*, 3: 29–48.

Form, W. (1982) 'Self-employed manual workers: petty bourgeois or working class?', *Social Forces*, 60: 1050–69.

Galbraith, J. (1967) *The New Industrial State*, London: Hamish Hamilton.

Gallie, D. (1988) 'Employment, unemployment and social stratification', in D. Gallie (ed.) *Employment in Britain*, Oxford: Blackwell.

—— (1991) 'Patterns of skill change: upskilling, deskilling or the polarization of skills?', *Work, Employment and Society*, 5: 319–51.

Gamarnikow, E. et al. (eds) (1983) *Gender, Class and Work*, London: Heinemann.

Gerry, C. (1985) 'Small enterprises, the recession and the "disappearing working class" ', in G. Rees et al. (eds) *Political Action and Social Identity*, London: Macmillan.

Gerth, H. and Mills, C.W. (1961) *Character and Social Structure*, London: Routledge and Kegan Paul (first published in 1954).

Giddens, A. (1979) *The Class Structure of the Advanced Societies*, London: Hutchinson (first published 1973).

—— (1985) 'In place of emptiness', *New Society*, 74: 383–4.

Gilbert, D. and Kahl, J. (1987) *The American Class Structure*, Belmont: Wadsworth (third edition).

Glass, D. (ed.) (1964) *Social Mobility in Britain*, London: Routledge (first published in 1954).

Glenn, N. et al. (1974) 'Patterns of intergenerational mobility of females through marriage', *American Sociological Review*, 39: 633–99.

Goldthorpe, J.H. (1972) 'Class, status and party in modern Britain: some recent interpretations, Marxist and Marxisant', *European Journal of Sociology*, 13: 342–72.

—— (1982) 'On the service class, its formation and future', in A. Giddens and G. MacKenzie (eds) *Social Class and the Division of Labour*, Cambridge: Cambridge University Press.

—— (1983) 'Women and class analysis: in defence of the conventional view', *Sociology*, 17: 465–88.

—— (1984) 'Women and class analysis: a reply to the replies', *Sociology*, 18: 491–9.

—— (1987) *Social Mobility and Class Structure in Modern Britain*, Oxford: Clarendon Press (revised edition, first published in 1980).

—— (1990) 'A response' in J. Clark et al. (eds) *John H. Goldthorpe: Consensus and Controversy*, London: Falmer Press.

Goldthorpe, J.H. et al. (1968) *The Affluent Worker: Industrial Attitudes and Behaviour*, Cambridge: Cambridge University Press.

—— (1969) *The Affluent Worker in the Class Structure*, Cambridge: Cambridge University Press.

Goldthorpe, J. H. and Bevan, P. (1977) 'The study of social

stratification in Great Britain', *Social Science Information*, 16: 279–334.

Goldthorpe, J. H. and Hope, K. (1974) *The Social Grading of Occupations*, Oxford: Clarendon Press.

Goldthorpe, J.H. and Lockwood, D. (1963) 'Affluence and the British class structure', *Sociological Review*, 11: 133–63.

Goldthorpe, J. H. and Payne, G. (1986) 'Trends in intergenerational class mobility in England and Wales 1972–1983', *Sociology*, 20: 1–24.

Goss, D. (1991) *Small Business and Society*, London: Routledge.

Gouldner, A. (1979) *The Future of Intellectuals and the Rise of the New Class*, London: Macmillan.

Gramsci, A. (1971) *Selections from the Prison Notebooks*, London: Lawrence and Wishart.

Grieco, M. (1981) 'The shaping of a workforce: a critique of the Affluent Worker study', *International Journal of Sociology and Social Policy*, 1: 62–88.

Hacker, H. (1951) 'Women as a minority group', *Social Forces*, 20: 60–9.

Hakim, C. (1980) 'Census reports as documentary evidence: the census commentaries 1801–1951', *Sociological Review*, 28: 551–80.

—— (1988) 'Self-employment in Britain: a review of recent trends and issues', *Work, Employment and Society*, 2: 412–50.

Hamilton, R. (1972) *Class and Politics in the United States*, New York: Wiley.

Harrington, M. (1984) *The New American Poverty*, New York: Holt, Rinehart and Winston.

Hauser, R. and Featherman, D. (1977) *The Process of Stratification*, New York: Academic Press.

Heath, A. (1981) *Social Mobility*, London: Fontana.

Heath, A. and Britten, N. (1984) 'Women's jobs do make a difference', *Sociology*, 18: 475–90.

Heath, A. and Evans, G. (1988) 'Working-class conservatives and middle-class socialists', in R. Jowell et al. (eds) *British Social Attitudes: the 5th Report*, Aldershot: Gower.

Heath, A. et al. (1985) *How Britain Votes*, Oxford: Pergamon.

—— (1987) 'Trendless fluctuation: a reply to Crewe', *Political Studies*, 35: 256–77.

—— (1988) 'Class dealignment and the explanation of political change: a reply to Dunleavy', *West European Politics*, 11: 146–8.

—— (1991) *Understanding Political Change: the British Voter 1964–1987*, Oxford: Pergamon.

Heisler, B. (1991) 'A comparative perspective on the underclass', *Theory and Society*, 20: 455–83.

Henry, S. (1982) 'The working unemployed: perspectives on the informal economy and unemployment', *Sociological Review*, 30: 460–77.

Hindess, B. (1973) *The Use of Official Statistics in Sociology*, London: Macmillan.

Hird, C. and Irvine, J. (1979) 'The poverty of wealth statistics', in J. Irvine et al. (eds) *Demystifying Social Statistics*, London: Pluto Press.

Hodge, R. W., Treiman, D. and Rossi, P. H. (1967) 'Occupational prestige in the United States 1925–1963' in R. Bendix and S.M. Lipset (eds) *Class, Status and Power*, London: Routledge and Kegan Paul (second edition).

Holmwood, J. M. and Stewart, S. (1983) 'The role of contradictions in modern theories of social stratification', *Sociology*, 17: 234–54.

Huaco, G. (1966) 'The functionalist theory of stratification: two decades of controversy', *Inquiry*, 9: 215–40.

Hudson, J. (1989) 'The birth and death of firms', *Quarterly Review of Economics and Business*, 29: 68–86.

Hyman, R. and Price, R. (eds) (1983) *The New Working Class? White Collar Workers and Their Organisations*, London: Macmillan.

Institute of Employment Research (1987) *Review of the Economy and Employment*, Coventry: University of Warwick.

International Labour Office [ILO] (1968) *The International Standard Classification of Occupations*, Geneva: ILO.

Irvine, J. et al. (eds) (1979) *Demystifying Social Statistics*, London: Pluto Press.

Johnson, H. (1973) *The Theory of Income Distribution*, London: Gray-Mills.

Katznelson, I. (1981) *City Trenches: Urban Politics and the Patterning of Class in the United States*, Chicago: University of Chicago Press.

Kelsall, R. and Mitchell, S. (1959) 'Married women and employment in England and Wales', *Population Studies*, 13: 19–33.

Kemeny, P. (1972) 'The affluent worker project: some criticisms and a derivative study', *Sociological Review*, 20: 373–89.

Kolko, G. (1962) *Wealth and Power in America: an Analysis of*

Social Class and Income Distribution, London: Thames and Hudson.

Krieger, J. (1986) *Reagan, Thatcher and the Politics of Decline*, Cambridge: Polity.

Ladd, E. (1989) 'The 1988 elections: continuation of the post-New Deal system', *Political Science Quarterly*, 104: 1–18.

Ladd, E. and Hadley, C. (1978) *Transformations of the American Party System*, New York: W.W. Norton (second edition).

Lash, S. and Urry, J. (1987) *The End of Organized Capitalism*, Cambridge: Polity.

Leete, R. and Fox, J. (1977) 'Registrar General's social classes', *Population Trends*, 8: 1–7.

Levy, F. (1987) *Dollars and Dreams: the Changing American Income Distribution*, New York: Russell Sage Foundation.

Lipset, S.M. (1963) *Political Man*, London: Heinemann.

—— (1969) *Revolution and Counter Revolution*, London: Heinemann.

—— (1991) 'American exceptionalism reaffirmed' in B. Schafer (ed.) *Is America Different? A New Look at American Exceptionalism*, Oxford: Clarendon Press.

Lipset, S.M. and Bendix, R. (1951) 'Social status and social structure', *British Journal of Sociology*, 2: 150–68 and 230–54.

—— (1959) *Social Mobility in Industrial Society*, Berkeley: University of California Press.

Lipset, S. M. and Zetterberg, H. L. (1956) 'The theory of social mobility', *Transactions of the Third World Congress of Sociology*, 3: 155–77.

Littler, C. and Salaman, G. (1984) *Class at Work*, London: Batsford.

Lockwood, D. (1989) *The Blackcoated Worker*, Oxford: Oxford University Press (second edition).

Loutfi, M. (1991) 'Self-employment patterns and policy issues in Europe', *International Labour Review*, 130: 1–19.

Lowe, G. (1987) *Women in the Administrative Revolution*, Cambridge: Polity.

Lupton, C. and Wilson, C. (1959) 'The social background and connections of top decision-makers', *The Manchester School of Economics and Social Studies*, 27: 30–51.

McDermott, J. (1991) *Corporate Society: Class, Property, and Contemporary Capitalism*, Boulder, CO: Westview Press.

MacKenzie, G. (1974) 'The "Affluent Worker" study: an evaluation and critique' in F. Parkin (ed.) *The Social Analysis of Class Structure*, London: Tavistock.

—— (1977) 'The political economy of the American working class', *British Journal of Sociology*, 28: 244–52.

McLellan, D. (1971) *The Thought of Karl Marx*, London: Macmillan.

McNally, F. (1979) *Women for Hire: a Study of the Female Office Worker*, London: Macmillan.

Macnicol, J. (1987) 'In pursuit of the underclass', *Journal of Social Policy*, 16: 293–318.

McRae, S. (1986) *Cross-class Families*, Oxford: Oxford University Press.

Mallet, S. (1975) *The New Working Class*, Nottingham: Spokesman.

Mann, M. (1973) *Consciousness and Action among the Western Working Class*, London: Macmillan.

Marsh, C. (1986) 'Social class and occupation', in R. Burgess (ed.) *Key Variables in Social Investigation*, London: Routledge and Kegan Paul.

Marshall, G. (1988) 'Classes in Britain: Marxist and official', *European Sociological Review*, 4: 141–54.

Marshall, G. et al. (1988) *Social Class in Modern Britain*, London: Hutchinson.

Marx, K. (1952) *Wage Labour and Capital*, Moscow: Progress Publishers.

—— (1969) *Theories of Surplus Value II*, London: Lawrence and Wishart.

—— (1970a) *Capital I*, London: Lawrence and Wishart.

—— (1970b) *Economic and Philosophical Manuscripts of 1844*, London: Lawrence and Wishart.

—— (1971) *The Poverty of Philosophy*, New York: International Publishers.

—— (1972) *The Eighteenth Brumaire of Louis Bonaparte*, Moscow: Progress Publishers.

—— (1974) *Capital III*, London: Lawrence and Wishart.

Marx, K. and Engels, F. (1848) *Manifesto of the Communist Party*, Moscow: Foreign Languages Publishing House, n.d.

—— (1962) *On Britain*, Moscow: Foreign Languages Publishing House.

—— (1970) *The German Ideology I*, London: Lawrence and Wishart.

Mattera, P. (1985) *Off the Books: the Rise of the Underground Economy*, London: Pluto.

Mayer, K. B. (1956) 'Recent changes in the class structure of the United States', *Transactions of the Third World Congress of Sociology*, London: International Sociological Association, 3: 66–80.

—— (1959) 'Diminishing class differentials in the United States', *Kyklos*, 12: 605–27.

—— (1963) 'The changing shape of the American class structure', *Social Research*, 30: 458–63.

Merton, R. (1968) *Social Theory and Social Structure*, New York: Free Press.

Miliband, R. (1973) *The State in Capitalist Society*, London: Quartet.

—— (1989) *Divided Societies*, Oxford: Oxford University Press.

Miller, S.M. (1960) 'Comparative social mobility', *Current Sociology*, 9: 1–89.

Mills, C.W. (1956) *White Collar*, Oxford: Oxford University Press (first published 1951).

—— (1967) *The Sociological Imagination*, Oxford: Oxford University Press (first published 1959).

—— (1968) *The Power Elite*, Oxford: Oxford University Press (first published 1956).

Moon, M. and Sawhill, I. (1984) 'Family incomes' in J. Palmer and I. Sawhill (eds) *The Reagan Record*, Cambridge, Mass: Ballinger.

Morris, M. (1989) 'From the culture of poverty to the underclass', *American Sociologist*, 20: 123–33.

Murgatroyd, L. (1982) 'Gender and occupational stratification', *Sociological Review*, 30: 574–602.

—— (1984) 'Women, men and the social grading of occupations', *British Journal of Sociology*, 35: 473–97.

Myrdal, G. (1944) *An American Dilemma*, New York: Harper.

Nichols, T. (1969) *Ownership, Control, and Ideology*, London: Allen and Unwin.

—— (1979) 'Social class: official sociological and Marxist', in J. Irvine et al. (eds) *Demystifying Social Statistics*, London: Pluto Press.

O'Connor, J. (1973) *The Fiscal Crisis of the State*, New York: St. Martin's Press.

Office of Population Consensus and Surveys [OPCS] (1980) *Classification of Occupations*, London: HMSO.

Ossowski, S. (1969) *Class Structure in the Social Consciousness*, London: Routledge and Kegan Paul.

Pahl, J. (1989) *Money and Marriage*, London: Macmillan.

Pahl, R. (1984) *Divisions of Labour*, Oxford: Blackwell.

Pahl, R. and Winkler, J. (1974) 'The economic elite: Theory and practice', in P. Stanworth and A. Giddens (eds) *Elites and Power in British Society*, Cambridge: Cambridge University Press.

Parkin, F. (1971) *Class Inequality and Political Order*, London: MacGibbon & Kee.

—— (1979) *Marxism and Class Theory: a Bourgeois Critique*, London: Tavistock.

Parsons, T. (1952) *The Social System*, Glencoe: Free Press.

Pawson, R. (1989) *A Measure for Measures: a Manifesto for Empirical Sociology*, London: Routledge.

Payne, G. (1990) 'Social mobility in Britain: a contrary view' in J. Clark et al. (eds) *John H. Goldthorpe: Consensus and Controversy*, London: Falmer Press.

Payne, G. and Abbott, P. (eds) (1990) *The Social Mobility of Women*, Basingstoke, Falmer Press.

Penn, R. (1981) 'The Nuffield class categorization', *Sociology*, 15: 265–71.

Penn, R. and Scattergood, H. (1985) 'Deskilling or enskilling? An empirical investigation of recent themes of the labour process', *British Journal of Sociology*, 36: 611–30.

Piachaud, D. (1982) 'Patterns of income and expenditure within families', *Journal of Social Policy*, 11: 469–82.

Piven, F. (ed.) (1991) *Labor Parties in Postindustrial Societies*, Cambridge: Polity.

Piven, F. and Cloward, R. (1982) *The New Class War*, New York: Pantheon Books.

Poulantzas, N. (1979) *Class in Contemporary Capitalism*, London: New Left Books.

Price, R. and Bain, G. (1983) 'Union growth in Britain: retrospect and prospect', *British Journal of Industrial Relations*, 21: 46 68.

Reid, I. (1989) *Social Class Differences in Britain*, London: Fontana (third edition).

Reid, I. and Wormald, E. (eds) (1982) *Sex Differences in Britain*, London: Grant McIntyre.

Renner, K. (1978) 'The service class', in T. Bottomore and P.

Goode (eds) *The Development of Capitalism*, Oxford: Clarendon Press (this article was first published in 1953).

Rex, J. and Tomlinson, S. (1979) *Colonial Immigrants in a British City: a Class Analysis*, London: Routledge and Kegan Paul.

Riddell, P. (1989) *The Thatcher Decade*, Oxford: Blackwell.

Roberts, H. (ed.) (1981) *Doing Feminist Research*, London: Routledge.

Robinson, R. and Kelley, J. (1979) 'Class as conceived by Marx and Dahrendorf: effects on income inequality and politics in the United States and Great Britain', *American Sociological Review*, 44: 38–58.

Roemer, J. (1982) *A General Theory of Exploitation and Class*, Cambridge, Mass: Harvard University Press.

Rogoff, N. (1953) *Recent Trends in Occuplional Mobility*, Glencoe: Free Press.

Rose, D. and Marshall, G. (1986) 'Constructing the (W)right classes', *Sociology*, 20: 440–5.

Ross, D. (1991) *The Origins of American Social Science*, Cambridge: Cambridge University Press.

Routh, G. (1987) *Occupations of the People of Great Britain, 1801–1981*, London: Macmillan.

Runciman, W. (1990) 'How many classes are there in contemporary British society?', *Sociology*, 24: 377–96.

Safilious-Rothschild, C. (1969) 'Family sociology or wives' family sociology', *Journal of Marriage and the Family*, 31: 290–301.

Sarlvik, B. and Crewe, I. (1983) *Decade of Dealignment*, Cambridge: Cambridge University Press.

Saunders, P. (1990) *Social Class and Stratification*, London: Routledge.

Savage, M. et al. (1992) *Property, Bureaucracy and Culture: Middle-Class Formation in Contemporary Britain*, London: Routledge.

Scase, R. and Goffee, R. (1980) *The Real World of the Small Business Owner*, London: Croom Helm.

—— (1982) *The Entrepreneurial Middle Class*, London: Croom Helm.

Schwendinger, J. and Schwendinger, H. (1971) 'Sociology's founding fathers: sexists to a man', *Journal of Marriage and the Family*, 33: 783–99.

Scott, J. (1982) *The Upper Classes*, London: Macmillan.

—— (1985) *Corporations, Classes and Capitalism*, London: Hutchinson (second edition).

—— (1991) *Who Rules Britain?*, Cambridge: Polity.

Sennett, R. and Cobb, J. (1977) *The Hidden Injuries of Class*, Cambridge: Cambridge University Press.

Shafer, B. (ed.) (1991) *Is America Different? A New Look at American Exceptionalism*, Oxford: Clarendon Press.

Singelmann, J. and Tienda, M. (1985) 'The process of occupational change in a service society' in B. Roberts et al. (eds) *New Approaches to Economic Life*, Manchester: Manchester University Press.

Smith, J. and Franklin, S. (1980) 'Concentration of personal wealth in the United States', in A. Atkinson (ed.) *Wealth, Income and Inequality*, Oxford: Oxford University Press.

Social Trends 21 (1991), London: HMSO.

Sombart, W. (1976) *Why Is There No Socialism in the United States?*, London: Macmillan (first published in 1906).

Sorokin, P. (1964) *Social and Cultural Mobility*, New York: Free Press (first published in 1927).

Stanworth, M. (1984) 'Women and class analysis: a reply to Goldthorpe', *Sociology*, 18: 159–70.

Stark, T. (1987) *Income and Wealth in the 1980s*, London: Fabian Society.

Steinmetz, G. and Wright, E. (1989) 'The fall and rise of the petty bourgeoisie', *American Journal of Sociology*, 94: 973–1018.

Stewart, A. et al. (1980) *Social Stratification and Occupations*, London: Macmillan.

Stinchcombe, A. (1989) 'Education, exploitation and class consciousness', in E.O. Wright (ed.) *The Debate on Classes*, London: Verso.

Storey, D. (ed.) (1983) *The Small Firm: An International Survey*, London: Croom Helm.

Szreter, R. (1984) 'The genesis of the Registrar-General's social classification of occupations', *British Journal of Sociology*, 35: 522–46.

Thompson, P. (1983) *The Nature of Work*, London: Macmillan.

Titmuss, R. (1962) *Income Distribution and Social Change*, London: Allen and Unwin.

Tocqueville, A. de. (1948) *Democracy in America*, New York: Knopf (first published in two parts 1835 and 1840).

Townsend, P. (1979) *Poverty in the United Kingdom*, London: Penguin.

Tumin, M. (1953) 'Some principles of stratification: A critical analysis', *American Sociological Review*, 28: 387–94.

—— (ed.) (1970) *Readings on Social Stratification*, Englewood Cliffs NJ: Prentice-Hall.

Vanneman, R. and Cannon, L. (1987) *The American Perception of Class*, Philadelphia: Temple University Press.

Veblen, T. (1963) *The Engineers and the Price System*, New York: Harcourt edn. (first published 1921).

—— (1964) *An Enquiry into the Nature of Peace and the Terms of its Perpetuation*, New York: Kelley (first published 1917).

—— (1970) *The Theory of the Leisure Class*, London: Allen and Unwin (first published 1899).

Walby, S. (1986) *Patriarchy at Work*, Minneapolis: University of Minnesota Press.

Walker, A. and Walker, C. (1987) *The Growing Divide*, London: Child Poverty Action Group.

Warner, W. (1960) *Social Class in America: an Evaluation of Status*, New York: Harper and Row (first published 1949).

Waters, M. (1991) 'Collapse and convergence in class theory', *Theory and Society*, 20: 141–72.

Watson, W. and Barth, E. (1964) 'Questionable assumptions in the theory of social stratification', *Pacific Sociological Review*, 7: 10–16.

Weber, M. (1961) *From Max Weber: essays in Sociology*, London: Routledge and Kegan Paul.

—— (1964) *The Theory of Social and Economic Organisation*, London: Collier-Macmillan.

—— (1968a) *Economy and Society I*, New York: Bedminster Press.

—— (1968b) *Economy and Society II*, New York: Bedminster Press.

—— (1968c) *Economy and Society III*, New York: Bedminster Press.

—— (1976) *The Protestant Ethic and the Spirit of Capitalism*, London: Allen and Unwin.

Westergaard, J. (1970) 'The rediscovery of the cash nexus', in R. Miliband and J. Saville (eds) *The Socialist Register 1970*, London: Merlin Press.

Westergaard, J. and Resler, H. (1975) *Class in a Capitalist Society*, London: Heinemann.

Williams, R. (1970) *American Society: a Sociological Interpretation*, New York: Knopf (third edition).

Winnick, A. (1989) *Toward Two Societies: the Changing Distri-*

butions of Income and Wealth in the U.S. since 1960, New York: Praeger.

Wood, S. (ed.)(1983) The Degradation of Work, London: Hutchinson.

Wright, E.O. (1976) 'Class boundaries in advanced capitalist societies', New Left Review, 98: 3–41.

—— (1978) Class, Crisis and the State, London: Verso.

—— (1979) Class Structure and Income Determination, London: Academic Press.

—— (1980a) 'Class and occupation', Theory and Society, 9: 177–214.

—— (1980b) 'Varieties of Marxist conceptions of class structure', Politics and Society, 9: 323–70.

—— (1985) Classes, London: Verso.

—— (1989) 'Women in the class structure', Politics and Society, 17: 35–66.

Wright, E.O. and Martin, B. (1987) 'The transformation of the American class structure 1960–1980', American Journal of Sociology, 93: 1–29.

Wright, E.O. and Singelmann, J. (1982) 'Proletarianization in the changing American class structure', American Journal of Sociology, 88: 176–209.

Zeitlin, I. (1989) The Large Corporation and Contemporary Classes, Cambridge: Polity.

Zweig, F. (1961) The Worker in an Affluent Society, London: Heinemann.

Name index

Subject index